EMPOWERMENT

How to stop pain and disease from taking over your life by connecting spirit, mind, and body

Dr. Stephanie E. Reid, ND, PhD
FOUNDER OF YOUR HEALING PLACE

Get inspired. Be empowered. Join the movement.
Book a free phone consult by going to
drstephanieyhp.com

Mention of specific companies, organizations or authorities in this book does not imply endorsement by the author or publisher. Nor, does mention of specific companies, organizations or authors imply that they endorse this book, its author or its publisher.

Medical Disclaimer:
This book is not intended to be a substitute for the medical advice of a licensed physician. The reader should consult with their doctor in any matters relating to his/her health.

Internet addresses and phone numbers in this book were accurate at the time it went to press.

First Edition July 2016
Second Edition January 2018

Dr. Stephanie E. Reid, ND, PhD
From Panic to Empowerment: How to embrace an angel when you expected a baby

ISBN-13:978-1983881817
ISBN-10:1983881813

Publisher Information Mailing Address: 3216 Batavia Ave, Baltimore, MD 21214* www.frompanictoempowerment.com

In Loving Memory of My Baby Sister

~*Taeisha Lester*~

2016

Acknowledgements

Rev. Dr. Medgar L. Reid, my husband, your support is unparalleled. Thank you for giving me the space to write. Your unconditional love gives fuel to my creativity. Date nights help fill in the gaps.

To my children: **Kevin, Kory, Diamonique, Megan, and Melody,** you all have inspired me to be as creative and free as I am. Watching you grow up gave me something to observe and learn from. Thank you.

Melody, it was your birth and death story that opened my heart to what God wanted me to hear… I'm still listening. Thank you for revealing the power of telling your story, which became rich content for the second book, From Panic to empowerment, How to embrace and angel when you expected a baby.

Table Of Contents

Acknowledgements

Before You Turn Another Page: Know that you will be transformed 1

Introduction 5

Chapter 1: It's you!..11

Chapter 2: The Name Of The Game Is Integration 23

Chapter 3: Tools of Engagement 39

Chapter 4: Self Exploration: How Do You Feel?.......................53

Chapter 5: Spirit Work: Acknowledging the Boss" 69

Chapter 6: Mind: Rewrite Your Story...81

Chapter 7: Body Talk: Renewal 105

Chapter 8: Spirit, Mind, Body Connected 123

Chapter 9: Alternative Methods for a Disease and Pain-Free Life 131

Chapter 10: Dr. Stephanie's Story 143

Conclusion...149

References 160

Table Of Contents

Before You Turn Another Page: Know that you will be transformed

Yes, really! Many books promise some form of profound shift after reading its contents. That's how you sell a book; get the Best Seller! I write with the same hopes of acknowledgment of my work and of course, I'd love to make the Best Seller's list. Yet, that is not the focus or even the reason for this work. The true, down dirty reason, is that I was hurting so bad, I needed to learn to connect with the inner parts of myself to find relief- before I lost my mind. My clients suffered too. How could I help myself, find the missing piece to end suffering and not share it with them?

That is why *you* will be transformed! It takes one to know one. I've felt your confusion, felt like my heart was ripped out of my chest and suffered much physical illness- many very serious.

Yet, there was always a reason why... I needed to understand the why. Why did I break down physically when I was at the lowest point in my emotional life? Was I alive at all or just breathing? These thoughts may sound eerily familiar. That's ok. It gets better!

Within these pages, I share my personal tidbits to drive points home. I even use actual scenarios of clients I've helped. Their names have been changed, yet the stories are real. They need to be real for you to see that you are not alone in your agony and you have a whole movement behind you searching for the same things you are... relief, wholeness, and happiness. I call it bliss.

You have not found your bliss yet, but you will. It's hidden at the moment because you have been taught not to trust your feelings, encouraged to swallow your pain and have old belief systems locked so deep within you can't see the way out. There is a golden door. It's there. I will show it to you by first intimately introducing you to your spirit, mind, and body. Then I will teach you how to reflect reframe and renew. It all goes together quite nicely- easy ~ peasy.

The Language: The language I use is not very conservative. I use terms that are familiar, yet not often used in formal writing. I did not see the need to connect with you as a scholar. I wish to connect with you person to person. So, the language is respectful, yet common. The tone of the book is as if you and I are friends and we're just having this wonderful conversation. Sharing truths with a friend I see in need.

Writing style: My style is all about making you able to flow with our conversation. There are imagery and sound effects that add drama to the points I feel have a greater impact adding shock factor. Some phrases will make you laugh, which makes the insight all the more poignant and retainable. Yes, I really want you to feel and connect with the lesson. I believe you will.

The online experience: This book's original content came from the online course: From Panic to Empowerment. The course came first because I needed to learn how to prepare information fast, on a platform that most are on anyway. Everyone is on the computer doing something. Giving my clients this information was my priority, I even gave away sample course access, Facebook discounts, and raffles. Somehow, I wasn't satisfied and wanted to make sure the same content could be found in a kindle forum, workbook, and even audio. I did mention this was a movement!

CONNECT WITH ME: I appreciate being in touch with my reader.

Facebook.com/ Frompanic2empowerment

Twitter.com/DrStephDr

MY WEBSITES: To learn more about my work:

drstephanieyhp.com

Frompanictoempowerment.com

Introduction

"Empowerment is one of those words that can be used for anything. Yet here it means feeling good about learning how to be responsible for your own well-being. In spite of what they are trying to tell you, you still have your God-given power to rise above adversity when you have the right information. Empowerment means learning the tools that lead to health happiness forged by wisdom. ~
Dr. Stephanie E. Reid

By reading this introduction, you will find the insight you are seeking contained in the pages of this book. I can say that with confidence. In my personal reading experience, I have found that when skipping the intro, I miss an opportunity to really grasp the full meaning of what is being presented.

Like many, I like things fast. I like getting to the root cause of problems so I can attack them - head-on. That way, I get quick tips and solutions to move onto the next adventure of my life.

However, what usually winds up happening is; I read the entire book - skipping the intro - then feel like I missed the point. As if a secret was hidden from me. That is frustrating!

Feeling stuck like that eats at me. Finally, after going all the way back to the beginning and reading the intro, I find myself saying under my breath, "Oh, *that* is what I was missing!"

To save you that agony, I will share with you briefly why I felt the need to write. I will explain why the information in these pages can create a shift for you. A shift that eases your spirit soothes your mind and relaxes your body so healing can begin.

Are you ready?

Good. Let's begin...

Over the past 10 years, I have helped many people see the benefits of taking care of themselves naturally. As a massage therapist, I successfully taught my patients the importance of releasing muscle tension and soreness. As a naturopath, I've encouraged others to recognize and utilize natural and alternative resources to improve health.

As a gerontologist, I've been able to explain the aging process and its effects on emotional and physical health outcomes.

However, through these experiences, I have learned that it's a moot point if my clients don't understand the importance of using natural medicine properly.
As we've all heard, natural medicine entails spirit, mind, and body connections. Sure, this sounds good, but how does one apply it consistently to achieve the best results?

This was the dilemma I faced with my clients.

As long as I was giving them something for the physical concerns and we talked about the spiritual and emotional issues - improvements happened.

Success was short-lived. I felt defeated and was afraid that they'd think natural medicine didn't work. My biggest concern was having those who believed in what I did... leave feeling hopeless.

From my years of experience, I've realized that people seek natural and alternative medicine when they have already tried (exhausted) conventional treatment with no success. Taking prescription drugs with side effects and having surgeries that leave scars can be hard to the spirit, mind, and body.

After thinking about my clients, a few observations came to light. There were two major concepts I needed to convey; 1) two weeks of feeling better doesn't mean healing is complete, 2) true healing can be their reality using natural medicine.

It is obvious that people are hurting; spiritually, emotionally and physically. With so many theories and truths circling, many are frustrated and feel like there is no hope. I hate to sound redundant about the hope, but that is what I see...

If you have picked up this book, you are one of those people. So I am speaking directly to you. Where you are right now, I have seen many get stuck right here.

The feeling of stagnation can create depression and severe anxiety. I struggled with this and hated feeling like that, so I loathe seeing others going through it.

I have always felt compelled to pull them out, sometimes to my own detriment. But now that you have been called out, this is for you!

Keep reading so you can get to the good part. You know... the part when the light bulb comes on and everything that you thought you knew is revealed, and you want to reach out and hug me! I am a hugger. Someday we shall meet, and there WILL be a big hug from me to you.

Let's get back to the why of this book...

Since we live in such a fast-paced society, we expect to feel better fast. If we feel better, the assumption is we are healed.

That idea isn't even close to the truth! We have the fast stuff with the western medical model, and people are still dying, suffering and waiting for ... relief.
So this is why this book was written - to give you relief; relief from the anxiety that creeps up and makes you feel horrible, without knowing why. I write to give voice to your silent suffering, from your inability to express your truth.

This book aims to fish out the true root causes of your health challenges. When you really understand that the power of healing lies within, and you have everything you need already to heal, you can be free to live the life that moves and flows from panic to empowerment.

Wow, that felt well didn't it?! Some truths just resonate and when they do you can get an immediate shift... to a higher place of feeling better.

In a nutshell, this book is your new feel-good tool. Yeah, you can begin to feel good when you see that you are not losing your mind. Your aches and pains, twitches and groans, all have a place.

So what is the missing link, the difference from any other "guru"?

Glad you asked...

The one piece added to this book unlike any other "self-help" model is...

I'll TEACH YOU HOW!

I will teach you how to connect your spirit, mind, and body by first dissecting each part (spirit, mind, and body). Then, I will help you perfect a simple 3 step tool that you can use to evaluate your experience, get to the root cause of the problem, and change your thinking about it; so your body can relax and heal.

Spirit, mind and body connections to health will no longer be a mystery that only monks can solve. And, you won't have to sit for hours in meditation (although, that practice will be discussed in later chapters).

What you will be doing is getting to know yourself. To do that, you must slow down to hear what your spirit is saying, what your mind is thinking and what your body is revealing.

Internalizing these truths will put you in the driver's seat of your life and your health. When you feel the power of being in charge of you, it will be very difficult for anyone to dictate what is best for you. You will be able to make new choices, pulling from the strength of being connected.

Lastly… if you haven't picked it up, this book was written to heal those who are truly hearing the call to go back to the basics.

Chapter 1: It's you!

Have you ever wondered why you are still suffering from the same pains and diseases, even though you've tried so many ways to get relief? Don't feel bad, most people have an arsenal of unused prescription drugs, lotions, creams, herbs and even some fancy contraptions.

You are still scratching your head about this because you are trying to get relief. And so far, nothing is working. I've had moments like that, and it really made me question myself and my sanity! Any suffering that lasts too long will make the sanest person feel unstable. If you are feeling a bit unstable right now, hold on. You *will* learn what you need to do to make a huge shift. I will share with you some really amazing concepts that you may not have ever considered. Once you understand and use these concepts the things that used to make the hair stand up on the back of your neck will make you laugh. Seriously!

One major reason why you, and so many others, are in this boat is that you keep parroting similar, "non-results" information. Most likely you have all of those remedies, potions, and pills because you got the information from a well-meaning friend, family member or even a doctor.

At the time, the information seems worth investigating and

even investing in. However, shortly after trying it and giving the remedy, drug or new device all of your attention and hope, you discover the relief you anticipated never came!

At this point, I can imagine how frustrated you must be. But, this is not the time to throw in the towel just yet! Why? Because I am very certain I have the tools you need to get the relief you deserve.

You see, I am no different than you. I too suffered from many things that I thought would surely take my life. I tried a lot of things and most only gave a temporary fix, only to haunt me later.

My story...

One day, I was sitting at my desk at work and thought I had a heart attack. Yeah; I was feeling as if I was having, a full-blown heart episode. I drove myself to the hospital and got every test known to man. My Blood Pressure was 220/190 – that was a huge concern. But every other test came back normal! My kidneys, liver, lungs, the colon was all good. So what the heck was going on? Keep reading...

Even though my blood pressure was reading *stroke*, my heart tests all came back normal too; but with an interesting twist. The picture of my heart showed a weird shape. In short, I was healthy, yet my heart was suffering from a "broken heart." If I were a cartoon character, my eyes would have appeared to boomerang out of my head when I heard the results.

The actual medical term is Takotsubo (Stress) Cardiomyopathy! Yeah, this phenomenon actually exists! Who knew? I sure didn't.

Hey, doctors don't know everything. I just gave you a big nugget. Did you catch it! In slow motion...."*Doctors don't know everything.*"

The reason why I shared that very personal story is to show you that there is one person you have not consulted with regarding your disease and pain. You trust the advice of your doctors (check the hint), your co-worker, an infomercial or even a magazine before you consult the only person that knows.

The only person that could give you the correct answer you totally dismiss; but you dress that source every day, feed it and even drive it around!

What is the source? You are the source!

It's you!

Yes! You read that correctly. YOU hold the secret to how to stop pain and dis-ease in your life. We all have that power. The problem is - few have the tools or the "know how" to tap into it.

When the nurse told me I had broken heart syndrome, I knew she was right. A few months earlier I had given birth to a beautiful baby girl. We named her Melody.

Melody passed away in my arms nine hours and twenty minutes after I gave birth to her, on my husband's birthday! But who knew heartbreak could create a real physical crisis? My spirit was confused, broken and devastated. ... Of course, I was heartbroken.

Most people don't give too much thought to how much pain and disease is a manifestation of the spiritual and mental processes that the body is just expressing. When I figured it out, I felt it was a MUST to share the information with as many people as possible could see the connection and get relief!

ASK YOURSELF....

So here in these pages, I am offering not only the tools to move you from panic to empowerment; but also insight into how not to have your life high jacked by disease and pain. Panic does not have to be your middle name, and you *can* get relief.

Getting relief from any pain or disease you are suffering from is possible. As you continue reading, I will share with you exactly what I mean.

In a nutshell, here it is. I call it the "3Rs Approach to Healing" - simple name, but powerful tool. If I'd say so myself, I think it is one of the most important "life hacks" you will learn to date.

If you know anything about hacking, you understand that it is a reference to mean doing something easier or more efficiently to make life simple. Who doesn't want the healing process to be simple?

Heck, these days, we all just want good health to be attainable. And… it is.

Once you learn the "3 Rs Approach to Healing", you will be

14

able to move from a state of panic and despair forward into a life that is meaningful and filled with actualized hope. Not just empty promises prescribed in a little brown transparent plastic bottle with a childproof top.

Truth be told, those prescription bottles should be cemented shut so nobody can open them. No medication on earth cures anything except antibiotics, which cures the infection. Medications just treat and treat and treat. Before you know it, you are taking more medications and then… you die.

There is no cure in that! You don't need to have twenty Ph.D.'s to figure that one out. Look around you. You know someone or a few who have traveled this dead-end road. Was it your grandparents, spouse or neighbors? This is the main reason why you are reading this book. You have seen the devastation and are at your wit's end, maybe locked in fear because you pray for a better outcome than what you have witnessed.

I digress… back to the 3 R's shall we?

The "3 R's Approach to Healing" is based on the premise that we are not just an ears nose, and throat, but a magnificent creation of our Creator that has three distinct character traits that make us who we are.

You, I, and everyone else have a spirit, mind, and a body. Some of us really get deep and over think this process. Many don't think about it at all. Yet we all must acknowledge *that* truth to harness the power of our own energy - to be healed or receive healing.

Western medicine has us all brainwashed into thinking that we are many pieces of flesh that just so happen to be in the same body. There is a specialist for your liver, kidney, heart, bones and even brain. The last time I checked my own body, all of my parts were together. If all of my organs are in the same body why is the western model concerned with my parts?

If you live in Maryland, and you have a heart problem, you will most likely go to Johns Hopkins Hospital to see a cardiologist. The cardiologist may discover a thyroid condition and will send you to an endocrinologist for treatment. The endocrinologist will send you to an orthopedist if you are having bone issues.

Now, even though these conditions are interrelated, often times the three specialists may or may not consult with each other regarding the best care for you. Since you don't know what to do, you don't even ask.

So now what you get is a sense of disconnection, confusion, and drug interaction side effects that none of your providers will admit to. After all, what he /she gave you was designed to treat the symptoms, not cure you.

If you complain about side effects, you will be looked at like you have three heads and two noses.

To continue on with this scenario, let's dig a bit deeper. You may begin to feel worse than you did before you saw any of those doctors. Yet, even your family condones the need for more medications, while you are slowly withdrawing in your spirit as if being sucked into a black hole.

The reason you feel so bad is that not only are you suffering physically, but your spirit is agitated, and your mind is being challenged to find a spot in reality that you can be comfortable with.

Meanwhile, nobody hears you spiritually, and your mind is being assaulted as you try to explain that you don't think the course of action is working. You become anxious and depressed, and the next provider sends you to a therapist for antidepressants. Sound familiar?!

In my humble opinion, I don't believe that the current system is designed to cure you or me. The word "cure" is protected as if it's a bad rumor about your mother. Nobody is allowed to say cure. The operative words and phrases are "treat," "may cause" or "studies have shown…" Since there is no real incentive to cure, there is no need to share with you that you are NOT just an ear, nose or throat patient.

You are a person with a spirit, with a mind that thinks, and a body that expresses itself based on the cues of those parts.

It would be far too easy to heal if you knew that truth. But, it's much more profitable to disconnect you and send you to various specialists to keep you in the dark about the truth.

The truth is…

Ready? Here it is right between the eyes; your third eye of higher knowing…
The truth is; your body was designed to heal itself. All you have to do is take away what it does not need and give it what

it does need!

Did that sound loud and obnoxious?
It was meant to!

You know this. I'm just reminding you…

As far as I am concerned, what you need right now to be truly whole is to be introduced to the other parts of yourself that have been estranged; so you can get acquainted with the business of healing.

You need all of you to engage in this process. The transformation begins with acknowledging your spirit. The work is done by changing old beliefs systems so your body can relax enough to begin healing.

That… is the premise of the 3 R's Approach to Healing.

A glimpse of the 3Rs Approach to Healing Disease and Pain. (Reflect, Reframe, Renew)

Reflect

Reflection requires that you stop, sit quiet, and check in. A quick evaluation of the emotions you feel will give a bird's eye view of your emotional state. Emotions are the language of the spirit. Your pain or disease comes from the discomfort of your spirit. Why is that? We are a spirit, housed in a body, with a mind that thinks, but the outward expression of the spirit and mind is felt in the body! Just as your joy and vitality come from a "happy place" – spirit. If you are suffering from chronic pain or have been diagnosed with a disease, check-in, evaluate your feelings. (spirit)Dig deep to find out if you feel happy, sad or agitated. The answer to that simple question will identify the 1st R. So, how are you feeling now?

Changing the perspective of how you view a situation or symptom will dictate your perception. Changing your perspective means making whatever spiritual or mental shift you need; to get to a place of feeling good. Keep in mind, this does not mean feeling good at the expense of someone else, but INSPITE of someone else.

> *"Your happiness is not found on the other side of any person, place or thing. Your happiness comes from within." -Emily Fletcher,*
> *Mind Valley Academy*

Reframe

Reframing the meaning of a circumstance is powerful! It creates an opportunity to re-write the old script and throw out old beliefs that no longer serve your idea of who you would like to become. This is your opportunity to drop kick some old baggage. Your way of doing things that makes you happy is perfectly fine. Who makes the rules? YOU DO! Discomfort comes in when you neglect your spiritual self in the name of going with the status quo. God has made you one of -a –kind, unique. You know when something does not feel right. So don't go along for the ride. Choose your own route. Many diseases and pain are caused by unresolved anger, fear, resentment, etc.

Renew

Renewal is what happens to the body when you successfully use the first 2 Rs. Reflection helps identify the origin – spirit. Reframing gives you permission to change your perception. Seeing things from a new light that is empowering allows the body to relax. As soon as the body relaxes from holding on to "old stuff," it begins the miraculous job of repairing itself. It's like the icing on a magnificent cake you are creating. I used a cake metaphor because it symbolizes celebration. Celebrate your breakthrough!

Renewal is so good because it is a passive by-product of Reflection and Reframing. When you have successfully learned the concept of the first 2 Rs, you'll know it.

How?

You will feel relaxed, calm, at peace... and in *love* with everything around you. Finding a happy place in your spirit sets the stage for healing. It's at that place when the body STOPS using its resources to deal with metabolic and biochemical issues relating to stress and shifts into healing and repair.

That is the moment when pain and disease begin to subside. Stress levels decline, allowing the body to shift gears for healing. The more often you use the "3Rs Approach to Healing" the more relief you can expect. Eventually, you will find that true healing is possible.

Adding other modalities will finally prove effective. Since you are a spirit, mind, and body- healing can never really be achieved without integration of all three.

Now, you have the tools to be pain and disease free!

Keep in mind that you must be vigilant that old habits don't creep in to steal your joy, bust your bubble or rain on your feel-good parade.

The profound advice I can offer you now is to practice the 3Rs with every single opportunity you can. Heck, practice on your family members or friends; after you have exhausted your own stuff - of course.

No, please don't go out masquerading as a sidewalk psychotherapist. But, yes... practice your understanding of how powerful you are by employing the "3Rs Approach to Healing". You can't fully practice until you have gone through the rest of the book to get the nitty-gritty details. But, practice is what will make your life feel like you have won the lottery.

Feel the possibilities, think about them let your body experience it...

By learning and practicing new skills, you will continue the transformational work of moving from Panic to Empowerment in not only your life but the lives of those around you. Now it's time...

Go forth and help yourself get connected to see the light, break free...

Hold it, hold it... stop for a second.

Don't get carried away, that was a trick. Did you catch it?

I gave you the quick version of what is required to move you from Panic to Empowerment. But that is NOT all of it.

Stopping here and not reading to the end will give you the same results you have always gotten. Let's do this right- this time. Take the time to dissect and learn these parts so when you do employ this awesome tool, you will be able to really internalize and maximize the potential for personal growth and wellbeing.

Whew...

That was close, I know. Don't be fooled.

After reading to the end, it will be impossible to get wrapped up in things that don't serve you completely (spirit, mind, and body). The quick fix is ALWAYS code for - don't believe the hype.

Although this is a simple, yet effective, approach to wellness you will only be scratching the surface of what is possible. The tips contained in this book are the cornerstone for moving you From Panic to Empowerment.

Exploration of this concept and harnessing the true power within can be achieved by enrolling in the 7-week online course From Panic to Empowerment: How to stop pain and disease from taking over your life by connecting spirit, mind, and body.

The seven-week self-paced course is designed to unlock the mystery of how healing is truly possible. At the end of this book, you will be given an invitation to enroll in the course that will finally put you in the driver's seat of your life to be able to experience the bliss of health and vitality.

Chapter 2: The Name Of The Game Is Integration

When you think about what it means to be healthy, I bet you imagine being pain-free, having high energy, and most of all, and a sense of true well-being. And this feeling stems from understanding and implementing a regimen that leads to complete wellness.

That sounds good, right? But it probably is not the case for you, at least not right at *this* moment. That is the main reason why you have this book in your hand. You want something better! Whether you have minor headaches or chronic disease, the same idea applies. You want a new reality...

You have probably already tried many things, and even achieved a level of relief, only for your symptoms to return!

Sometimes, symptoms return in a gentle whisper gradually increasing in intensity. Or, they return like a freight train, knocking you out for the count. You gasp!

"Well damn, I really didn't see that coming!"

Life is like that. Often times it may feel like things are happening *to* you, and you are just a bystander, instead of the *creator* of your circumstances. When that happens, you panic; wondering, what the heck is happening to me?

When we are not actively participating in our own lives and really making proactive choices, we fall prey to the status quo. We vicariously live through the decisions of others, gliding on the wind of another's sail, so to speak. Although we sometimes *wake* up just in time to change course; often times, we wake up in the middle of the "nightmare" frantically stumbling for the nearest exit.

Once you realize it's time to do something different, you have to be sure you have the best information to pick the "right" exit for your circumstance.

That, my friend, is Empowerment! Empowerment is when to leap into your bliss and having all the right equipment to do so. No matter what it looks like to anyone else.

So what does it mean to jump into your bliss? Bliss means extreme happiness among other things, depending on the context of thought you are trying to convey. Here the main thought is happiness. When you are courageous enough to make decisions that are right for you, even when others think you're crazy; that's happiness-bliss. Being able to make your own decisions is extremely liberating. Even if the result does not turn out exactly as you had hoped.

At least it is *your* decision, and you can feel good about taking a stand. When you allow someone else to make decisions for you; you have someone to blame if things don't work out. Blame is self-defeating and adds more fuel to the fire of disease. Finding your own bliss on the other hand - gives you power, and lifts your spirits so high that the downwind of negative energy barely has an impact on you. ☺

That is bliss.

To follow your bliss, however, requires courage and needs a plan. I'm sharing this with you early in the book because this courage will be the same energy needed to disregard ideas that have kept you unwell.

You see, wellness is not something that you can touch as a table or a chair. It is intangible energy that drives you forward, while illness and disease will pull you into a cocoon. Even though you may not like it, you remain there because it's familiar.

After reading this book, not only will you be able to embrace your bliss, you will be able to help others find theirs. Learning the "3 Rs Approach to Healing" technique is easy. Its application is practical and can be used in a few seconds. Mastering the technique will give you your power back to harness your bliss to heal- spirit, mind, and body.

It's about feeling good

When we feel good physically, everything seems to be in place. Our spirits are high, we're thinking good thoughts, and everything is "right" with the world. Yet, when we feel bad (pain, anxiety, disease) we rarely trace the same thought back to our spirit, mind, body connection. Instead, we compartmentalize ourselves and only deal with what we know.

Let me explain. If your foot hurts, your foot hurts. "How do I fix my foot?"

Your foot becomes your only focus.

Fixing your foot becomes the dominant thought. If you just stubbed your toe, that's one thing, but what if the pain is chronic? This chronic condition (foot pain, as our example) can stem from a complication of diabetes, nerve damage, or arthritis. But all you can identify is foot pain, so you invest more energy in dealing with the foot pain.

The wheel keeps turning. Some resolve happens, but the pain continues until you say to yourself, "There has got to be something else!"

There is something else! It's the holistic approach, that alternative healing stuff you've heard about.

It's the Spirit, Mind, Body connection thing… right!?

RIGHT!

Yes…the alternatives are there. But, be honest, do you really want to feel good?

Or are you just saying it to get along?

Follow this train of thought…

When we aren't feeling good, we downplay it. We dismiss it, and we may even ignore it. Worst of the worse, we swallow our pain and discomfort as if it represents a badge of honor. We may even become a martyr, suffering to make other's life easy.

So we lie to others and to ourselves about what is really going on. But by the time the cat hits the fan, we are in full-blown crisis- cancer, heart attack, stroke...dead.

CASE STUDY:

There was a sweet young woman that I knew for many years. Her life was filled with tragedy and trauma. Due to her father's indiscretions, her mother left them. The girl was very giving and supportive to all of her family and friends. She occasionally mentioned that she felt abandoned and alone. She would open up a bit to allow her deepest hurt to show, but would quickly dismiss her feelings.

During one of our chats, she recants a time that she felt the most alone when her father was murdered. Her mother had already left, and she felt there was no one in the world to care for her. As she opens her heart and tells her story, she shares that she never really felt loved, but she knew that no matter what, God would take care of her.

After many years of getting to know this young woman, she confided in me that she was stricken with breast cancer. Her strain of cancer was very aggressive, and it moved through her body like a brush fire in a dry forest with 50 miles per hour winds. As her cancer spread from her breast to her lungs, she suffered from pain all over her body. However, she continued to give to others, even when she could no longer speak and in doing so, she did not accept the help that she advocated for others. Even during cancer treatments in Mexico, she continued to be a support system for others.

During her last days, she continuously suffered and finally

gave herself permission to say, "I need help now, take me to the hospital." As she took her last breath, she suffered from severe anxiety and despair. It was as if she was fighting death and was afraid to embrace the peace of being pain-free.

When we are used to suffering, we don't always see the escape hatch that God has placed in front of us, whether in the form of pain management, or around the clock care. If we don't feel worthy, the unworthiness (learned behavior), if not dissected and put in its place, will dictate our life's choices even in our last days.

As I think about the young woman, I am still perplexed as to why she did not fight for herself as hard as she fought for others. She did not give herself permission to be taken care of by hospice, nurses, or health care providers until she could no longer stand the excruciating pain in her emaciated, frail frame.

She suffered in the name of, "it's not that bad… I'll beat this… God has a plan for me… I'll get better." I wonder if on a subconscious level whether she even felt worthy of the care that was required to maintain her life. She had given so much to others from an empty vessel. Maybe, she did so in hopes that someone would give it back. I pray for that young woman daily.

Why does this happen? I really don't KNOW, but I can speculate that these are subconscious cues playing themselves out from the stories we've told ourselves about our past.

Psychologists say that between birth to age seven, children are highly impressionable. Whatever mess they are exposed to is engrained in their minds and is displayed in their behavior.

A SCENARIO:

So let's say you saw your parents argue, and it frightened you. The loud voices may have sparked a sense of fear in you so great that every time you hear people, even speaking loudly, your heart races.

Now the story you must have told yourself was... "since my parents are loud, they must not like each other. If they don't like each other, and they made me, they must not like me either."

So what do you do?

You avoid verbal confrontation for fear of it meaning you are not liked. As a result, you learn to swallow your anger, frustrations, and fears. You don't let them out. Eventually, they manifest into, aches and pains in the stomach, then ulcers, then colitis, then colon cancer, then... well, you know!

All of this could have potentially been avoided if you were able to recognize that the original story you told yourself - way back when- does not have the same meaning in your adult life.

Speaking your truth is a good thing, as long as it is done with love. You speak your truth with love by first solidifying your intent. Communicate with the intention to be understood and to clarify your emotions. Then, realize that whatever response you get, you don't have to own it and it does not define you. When you don't speak your truth, the consequence is pain and disease.

Why? Because... Everything is centered on communication - verbal and non-verbal.

Being afraid to speak up leaves you vulnerable to both emotional and physical discomfort. When you cannot communicate your feelings, needs or discomfort; they don't disappear, they get buried. Eventually, they slip out manifesting in emotional blocks, unexplained illnesses, and strained relationships.

Panic sets in and you get swallowed up into your cocoon.

Playing the Game
Believe it or not, you play games with yourself when you experience disease. You create an entire conversation about what you perceive is happening. A few common phrases come to mind like...

"Maybe, if I just stop thinking about it, that horrible thing will go away."

"Time heals all wounds."

"My migraines have nothing to do with my thoughts."

Or, the common plot twist, you totally ignore your own issues and focus on the shortcomings of others to forget about your own. This may not be a conscious thing, but you do it (we all have done it).

This rarely works because after a while, the focal point of your deflection winds up becoming your own reflection and you get slapped in the face with your own reality.

Ouch!

Playing these games help for a while because you give yourself some leverage, but as time passes nothing really gets better. This is the time to get real with yourself and dig deep into the root cause of the emotion causing your disease.

Whether its foot pain or cancer, kidney failure or acne; there is a way to true healing. And the way is by cutting through emotional disillusionment!

CASE STUDY

A few years ago I had the pleasure of meeting a middle-aged man trying to get help for his wife. She was suffering from, what he thought was, a heart problem. Since she was very secretive, he wasn't sure what was going on, but he knew something was up. He would snoop when she was on the phone with her cardiologist. He came to see me because he just wanted his wife to be healthy and requested that I do the normal Naturopathic work up. At the time, it included the NanoSrt Stress Reduction therapy scan and laser treatment. Also, hair would be sent to the lab to determine if any mineral imbalances were contributing to her disease.

As I observed the husband, I noticed he had a very controlling demeanor, and it quickly became clear that his desire for his wife to see me was more about deflecting his own personal issues than helping her. It was as if he was using his appearance of concern as a way to control the parts of his wife that he apparently didn't feel he had access to. When his wife expressed her displeasure with him treating her openly disrespectful, he would become childlike as if he was the wounded party.

Observing the man further, I also noticed that the very same thing that agitated him about his wife was the same behavior he displayed. Watching this couple interact was quite an experience for me because I knew they had no idea what I was witnessing.

The way they danced around each other's comments with clever comebacks and snide remarks was amazing. They had mastered their game and played it well. Yet, both of them seemed to tolerate their relationship, not thrive on it.

The game is easy because everyone else plays it with us. By default that thought process is... "Nobody wants to hear my story anyway."

That may be true, yet at some point, you have to realize that it's the story that is creating the dis-ease. The sooner you identify it, reframe it and really look at the impact of the belief system that fed it; the sooner you can be empowered.

I actually heard a high "C" note as I typed E-M-P-o-w-e-r-ed.

Say it out loud! E-M-P-o-w-e-r-ed...

Wow, that sounded and felt good.

Feel the energy that comes with it.

Words have power!

In the case study, the husband learned to get his way with people by manipulating them into giving him what he wanted by acting childlike. His strange behavior would be seen as irritating to the victim of his antics, but it became an effective method of controlling situations that he felt locked out of. His most used phrase... "I'm ok; I just want her to be ok because I know she has a problem that she won't tell me about."

Empowerment is one of those words that can be used for anything. Yet here it means feeling good about learning how to be responsible for your own well-being. In spite of what they are trying to tell you, you still have your God-given power to rise above when you have the right information. Get the real information about how to be healthy, happy and wise. Join the Movement From Panic to Empowerment!

As you learn truths about your belief systems that have been holding you back, you can see that you have been accepting things as they are. Living life unfulfilled, slowly backing into the safe, yet dangerous cocoon.

The Cocoon
I thought it may be a good idea to touch on the idea of a cocoon. The formal definition is concerned with the larvae of insects; butterfly, moth or spider eggs. Here the definition fits more closely with the verb application, and I am using it to give imagery for how we close ourselves off in a protective stance, not letting our emotions out or healing in.

Shutting down is a way we play games with ourselves. Yet this "game" is more subconscious. You see, if we are going to truly heal the spirit, mind, and body, we must acknowledge when we are shutting our spirits down. The spirit is the feeling center. Who wants to feel when all you feel is hurt?

The hurt can be so darned overwhelming that you feel the only way to escape is to hide. The hiding begins gradually. Energy is zapped because of the adrenal gland, which responds to stress. The gland gets overworked causing spikes of energy from sodium released from the adrenal cortex.

If that mechanism is triggered too often, adrenal fatigue sets in. The fatigue translates into low energy, then low mood. This dance of low energy and low mood will also cause fluctuations in behavior.

Soon one finds themselves in a stress loop that creates tension in relationships; work, home, etc. These strained relationships create the need to hide. Often times a person will begin to feel like, "what's the use?" When you are spiritually and mentally exhausted, a physical expression will manifest itself to give you feedback on what is happening.

You often only see the physical.

By only seeing the physical the symptoms really never go away, they just give rise to signals that are more pronounced. The additional alarm reactions can be stopped in their tracks if you learn for yourself that when your BODY has given a signal, the spirit and mind are in crisis.

Potentially, this can be a dangerous place to be for the simple fact that low energy, low mood patterns are indicative of the biochemical makeup of those who would commit suicide.

Also, a person with this biochemical pattern is usually one that eats carbohydrate for energy, unable to eat proteins and fats without experiencing some form of gastrointestinal disturbance and is under a lot of stress. The stress can be physical or emotional. When the pattern lasts for long periods of time, exhaustion happens.

At that point, no amount of sleep or vacation time can correct the level of fatigue.

This experience can only be corrected with time and proper diet to ensure absorption of minerals and vitamins for the healing of the energy system on a cellular level.

This process takes time.

Additionally, if you are fatigued and you do not understand how you got there and how to get better, the hiding may turn into secret vices such as drinking and/or drug use to get the "edge" back.

We live in a society where it's seen as a sign of weakness to be tired, need a break or admit that enough is enough. We call the military veteran a hero when he/she has served several tours of battle, but we neglect to factor in the level of emotional and psychological stress they experienced. Then, we scorn the homeless veteran for finding a home in the gutter begging for food.

Acceptance
Learning to accept the fact that you are spirit, mind, and body will change the way you heal and seek to heal. It will relieve panic and stress, and help maximize the potential that once you find relief, you will keep it. Each time you feel discomfort, you should be able to STOP to reflect (spirit) on the potential origin, reframe (mind) the meaning of the experience to release stress and tension that is ultimately creating the discomfort (body).

If used often, this (3) three-step process will save you a lot of money, seeking specialist after specialist. You will gain a sense of true empowerment when you realize that this is *your* life, and can have complete control of your health and healthcare. As you discover the hidden causes, (spirit, mind, and body), you will be able to make informed choices on which practitioners to seek. Taking a more active role in your life will ensure that you will decide what you allow and what you will not. You have choices you know! Yes, please… ask more questions- take your power back!

Also, you will be able to discern whether you are willing to have your body polluted by poisonous drugs, invasive surgeries, and unnecessary diagnosis. That is what it means to be truly healthy from the inside out. Having the freedom to choose from a place of awareness of who you really are is an amazing realization.

Are you only an ears, nose and throat?! No, indeed! You are a completely integrated, magnificent person connected spirit, mind, and body. You can be empowered here in these pages to embrace that oneness to make it "work" for you, not against you.

I challenge you here and now to continue reading, get more insight, anticipate your new sense of freedom...

Chapter 3: Tools of Engagement

Get a personal journal. Be ready to Reflect, Reframe, and Renew; one part of yourself at a time. Let's do it!

When you really want something, it's because you have come to some realization that having it will change your life for the better. You want more money because you believe it will solve financial burdens and make room for more freedom to do other things.

However, with more money comes more responsibility in maintaining the wealth, as well as making sure you have investments in place for long-term growth. In a perfect world, you can amass wealth and not be burdened by taxes, audits and other people trying to concoct ingenious ways of helping separate you from your money.

But we are not in a perfect world.

I used that analogy to give a familiar connection with the concept I am trying to make.

When we seek help for health problems, you do so, not when there is a gentle alarm such as a headache or a sporadic sharp pain, but when you are faced with a life or death situation; or at least a chronic condition that can lead to death.

It's at that critical moment, you realize that life is precious, and you want to maintain it at any cost. That is a cost even wealth can't cover. Yet, you want health without taking responsibility for getting it as much as you desire financial security but don't have a clue how to maintain it.

Being truly free from disease is not just about the absence of pain, but includes a quality of life that has a connection with spirit, mind and body concepts. Health is a dance between these three parts of who we are.

When one is off, surely, it is just a matter of time before the other two components will begin to show signs of disease. When you are faced with these concepts that are presented right here, you scoff at the potential for healing to take place, because you have been lead to believe that ...well, something this profound should be more complicated.

But here lies a sobering reality. When you get to this point that you are literally fighting for your life; simple and easy can be profound and life sustaining!

It is at this moment that you realize that you don't have the correct tools to get the job done. But if you did, you'd want them to be easily accessible, user-friendly and intuitive.

You need tools to connect you with a reality you can embrace.

Here they are…

Using these tools will ensure that you get the most out of this content to be able to take action for your own success!

Step#1

Get yourself something really special to write on. Buy yourself a fresh journal. Consider the ones with a leather cover and a hard spine. Leather denotes quality and oozes "I'm important." You are the most important person in the world to you, or at least you should be. If you are not feeling quite that confident, don't worry. By the time we finish, you will. And you will want to thank me later for insisting that you make yourself important, #1.

Writing in a journal gives you mental space. It's like clearing out your closet of old clothes to make room for nice new ones. You can't get new stuff in the closet between your ears if you have old dusty belief systems and stories that only create clutter and confusion.

So, journaling will be your "mental closet," spring clearing event. Or … winter, fall or whatever season event you'd like to think of it as. The point is there is magic in clearing things out. If you really want to be released from your pain and disease, get a journal.

Step#2

Creating a ritual helps reinforce the importance of your goal to be disease and pain-free. Make the process special. There is nothing as nice as the feel of a new, seriously elegant, pen. I'd even get it engraved. After all, this pen will be the tool with which you unlock your mind and unleash your potential for healing. It is the key to your Empowerment. As you put pen to paper, you will see your life unfold like never before.

Just as I am doing now!

For years, I said I'd write a book. As you are reading, I am doing it... putting pen to paper (typing on my keyboard) and making my thoughts come alive. I am helping you heal and seeing my own transformation in the process. Writing is a very profound way to unlock ourselves.

I can actually hear myself thinking and taking dictation as I am sharing this with you. The more I write, the more inspired I become. I am empowered to say what it is that needs to be said to help you. As I continue on this train of thought, I think I am helping you, but in fact, I am the one being liberated to tell my truth, release my pain to heal my life... Thank You!

Step#3
Self-reflection requires a calm place to be able to go deep. True healing requires work. Personal work requires concentration. Find some good concentration music that sets the stage for good introspection. Now that you have the special music find your sacred location.

A place where you can feel like you can be free to write and think and even shed tears if that's what it comes to. Sometimes we need to shed tears for ourselves. Tears are a way to cleanse the soul and no matter how ugly and wet your face becomes you always feel better after you cry.

Whether you get to feel lighter in the mind or heart or whether it lulls you to sleep- don't miss a healing potential of a good cry.

The exercise of journaling will bring out hidden emotions, and that can be scary. But it will also offer "aha" moments of clarity. In essence, it is a small yet significant practice that can move you ever so gently from panic to empowerment.

The "3 R's Approach to Healing" is about finding the hidden beliefs that are driving the physical disease. Journaling is the tool that will give you that piece of the puzzle to create your healing masterpiece of empowerment.

Tools of Engagement

Step#1:
New Journal book
  ➢ separate into (3) section (spirit, mind, body)

Step#2:
Get a special pen to use in your new journal.
  ➢ No scratch paper your thoughts are sacred!

Step#3:
Set aside a special place.
  ➢ Special room

Step#4:
Choose a private space for journaling.
  ➢ Dedicated space any where

Step#5:
Set a time to be present.
  ➢ Same time daily

Where ever you decide to create your sacred space, make a commitment to be present when you go there. Decide that this is the place that you can be you, find you, or become the person that you desire to be.

Decorate it.

Give it a personal touch that embodies the energy you are to become.

Colors have energy. Even if you may not understand the meaning of the colors, you know how you feel in the colors. So just feel your way into decorating your personal space. That, in itself, is a very profound way to learn about you.

When you do settle on colors, investigate color meanings. You will be amazed at how your subconscious guided you into what you needed from the very colors you chose.

Step#4
Getting to know yourself requires private moments in a private space. You deserve all of the attention and more. But what if you don't have the luxury to create an entire private room? Clearing off a shelf or a desk that you can designate as your spot is just as good. You don't need a lot of space just room for your opulent leather journal and gorgeous engraved pen and you. Music is optional.

Step#5
When are you going to release your thoughts to paper?

Mornings, before you start your day?

Afternoon lunch break?

Saturday evening? Or, Sunday morning?

The beauty of this answer is that you have the freedom to choose!

But...

Be consistent. DO NOT PANIC if you get off track. Changing time and day may be necessary, but NEVER use pieces of paper in place of your special journal book, or use a pencil.

Your original thoughts on paper are sacred. Use them for healing. Being consistent with your private time will put your family on notice that you are doing important work. If you are organized and consistent with time and space, others will learn to respect your time and space. That small change can create a huge shift in your stress levels that can put a big dent in your experience of pain and disease.

Let's sit here in this space and think about time. There are only 24 hours in a day, and we all get the same 24 hours.

No one gets more or less time.

It may seem that way if time management is an issue. So setting a time sets *the time* for you to give yourself time. I know that is a lot of times, but to bring this point home, if you don't make time -there will be no good time.

Think about all the other things you make time for, even sometimes begrudgingly. Be honest. You do far more for others when you don't even feel like it. Take the energy and use it for yourself sometimes –pun intended!

Once you've completed these 4 steps, you are signaling to the universe that you are ready to heal. When you have completed those steps, go look in the mirror; give yourself a big hug and say, "I love you."

Now close the door labeled "Panic" and open the door to "Empowerment"...

Welcome!

Journal Reflection: How much effort do you expend getting to know others? Do you give yourself half of that time?

How Long Have You Had This Problem?

When you decide to take action for better experiences, it means you are serious about seeing a change in some area of your life. Knowledge is power... or better... the application of knowledge is empowering.
Reading and learning the wisdom contained in these pages will help you get to another level of your potential for healing. But first, let's consider what you are trying to get relief from and how long you've had this problem?

We live in a society that demands everything yesterday. We have microwave lives, internet relationships, and instant gratification syndrome. So when you really consider the length of time you have had pain or disease; the real question is how long have you actually been working a plan to get relief?

If you think about the many prescription drugs you may have taken; drug therapy would not actually qualify.

Taking pain meds is not designed to get rid of the origin of the pain (which is the definition of pain-free in this instance). Instead, its action is to cap off pain receptors, so you no longer feel the pain. Unfortunately, the root cause is still firing signals to your brain that something is wrong.

You are just shut out from experience and can't feel it. The fire is still burning, but the battery has been taken out of the smoke detector so to speak.

Even if you combine the above intervention with surgery, the same idea applies. The offending organ has been taken out, yet smoldering still exists, and it's just a matter of time before all hell breaks loose in your body, and every damned thing starts hurting.

What do you do then, when the ready–get-it-fast- remedy doesn't work?
You can't actually give up! What is possible is just around the corner.

You know the old saying it's always darkest before the dawn. So don't quit! (I believe I learned a poem of the same title when I was a kid…)

Alright, you must be thinking, "I haven't quite yet, I'm still reading…" Good!

I'm glad you're still with me. There is another option you may not have thought of.

That's why I wrote this little book and created an entire seven (7) week online course just so YOU could get some relief finally.

The give-me-relief- now recipe has lost its flavor. It doesn't even taste good anymore. The thought of surgery used to sound like sweet music to the sufferer's ears, but after the broken promises and inconsistent results, no one is happy to hear that option. It carries so much fear and uncertainty. Drugs have so many disclaimers it's hard to know if you should or shouldn't take them. The commercials are so inviting with nice music and gorgeous actors.

You can easily get sucked into the dream only to have your

hopes crushed by the disastrous disclaimers.

"… May cause bleeding ulcers, blindness, bladder cancer and baldness; ask your doctor if this (statin drug, steroid, pain medication) is right for you."
You hear this and watch the graphics and ask yourself, "Did I just see that, are my ears playing tricks on me… this is crazy." Yes, this is crazy!

There is a unique approach you can take. I have developed it through observation of others and trial and error on myself. Suffering does not discriminate. Everyone experiences it. Some of us climb out of the ditch while others stay a bit longer.

Disease and Pain Relief Finally!

The longer you allow yourself to experience pain and disease, the more likely there is a hidden benefit. There is a payoff for all of us for the discomfort in our lives.

Most often it is a deep subconscious pay off. The sneaky, yet powerful subconscious mind conversation goes something like this... "The more, I am unable to do for myself, the more help I will get."

Sometimes playing into that subconscious conversation may backfire. If you do not get the help or attention you feel you deserve, you will feel defeated. Instead of pulling yourself up, you manage to sink deeper into despair.

Being in a chronic state of disease and pain is not fun. But on a deeper level, we hope it will get us the attention we feel we deserve. In actuality, the real cry is from the inner child trying to get the attention of the grown-up for healing and wholeness.

A sobering thought is no one really hears your cry unless you verbally express it. How often can you really put into words what you may be going through?

Few people have the gift of mind reading. We hope people can read our minds. That way we don't have to muddle through the awkwardness of finding the right words.
Words are so inadequate…

We get angry at our spouse when they don't read our minds. After all, they should know you right?! Wrong.

People only know what you share. If you don't know what's in your subconscious, how will anyone else know? Let's put the inner child on notice that you are listening and are willing to re-connect!

Hint: This would be another good place to journal…

Now that you have been prepped, given a glimpse of the transformative content, get inspired! Get your special journal, pen, sacred space. In a few short weeks, you will move from Panic to Empowerment and be on your way to a

"I get a lot of sympathy from suffering and I don't have to be as responsible for other things. I can even neglect my part in creating this experience. Who deliberately wants to be filled with pain and disease? I didn't create this myself?! I am entitled to feel what I feel. My feelings are valid. I take care of everyone; it's time for someone to take care of me. Besides, this is the only way to get my needs met. When I'm healthy, I get ignored."

wonderful transformation of YOU!

Follow Through... A Word of Advice

You will always feel good when you are starting something new. Your energy is high, the mood is bright, and your mental clarity is on point. But, after a few weeks or less; other things get in the way, and you may begin to lose sight of the prize.

Why does this happen?

It happens when you don't commit to the transformation. Something will sidetrack you, seem more important, and before you know it; you missed a day, a week, then you give up. Shortly after, you feel defeated, and the small progress you made goes out the window. The potential progress you could make turns to hope un-received.

Let's be proactive this time. You must decide here and now to make the commitment to yourself to be the change you want to see and experience.

Nowhere in history has any great personal change comes without work, commitment to that work, and courage that allows you to step over hurdles that sidetrack what you are here to do. You are here, in this lifetime, to grow and be the best version of yourself. That will require work!

The past few pages were designed to fluff you up with love and compassion. These few paragraphs are designed to toughen you up! You can't give up or give in now. You can't afford to. Everything you have done until this very moment has only served to take the battery out of your smoke detector.

Take a good sniff… the fire is still burning, and you are only a few experiences away from choking from the debilitating signs of your pain and disease.

So, yes… Doing all of the steps from getting a journal to creating the time is all a part of staying focused. If you do any task for 21 days, it becomes a habit. Commit to journaling for 21 days. Learn to use the "3 Rs Approach to Healing" to move from Panic to Empowerment. By doing so, you will fortify and exponentially secure your transformation. Putting panic on notice that pain and disease will not take over your life, you will learn and master the tools necessary to connect your spirit, mind & body into your health equation for wholeness!

Chapter 4: Self Exploration: How Do You Feel?

There is a dangerous game we play with ourselves in the name of not wanting to appear to be a perpetually negative person.

What do we do?

We negate and deny everything we feel; especially if the feeling does not meet the requirements for other people's approval.

Essentially, we tell lies!

I lied!

Your therapist, friend or own spirit asks, "Nancy, how do you feel now that you have lost your job, buried your child, survived childhood sexual abuse, spousal abuse, two failed marriages and low self-esteem?"

You (Nancy) reply…

"Oh I'm fine, I will get through it. I overreacted, it wasn't that bad."

Lie, lie, lie, lie and lie!

We lie to ourselves.

Others asked, out of concern, can't believe their ears. They may whisper under their breath, "She/he is in denial."

And that is what you are - in denial.

The more you deny yourself the opportunity to explore your emotions and feel them, the less likely you will be able to accept your own feelings or trust yourself. That internal feedback is your spirit's way of guiding you into your bliss or away from danger. When you lose your ability to trust your spirit (feelings), you lose the opportunity to grow.

Any experience that reinforces your need to hide your feelings will contribute to tearing down your sense of self-worth, your ability to think or even your resolve to survive.

I can recall a period in my own life when all hell was breaking loose. My now ex-husband would often come home just as the birds started chirping. I didn't know whether he was dead or alive. The most likely explanation would be he was pulled for extra duty at the barracks. But his behavior would reveal my biggest heartbreak!

Instead of approaching me with a humble explanation, he'd shout and throw a tantrum. He was obviously feeling guilty about whatever he was doing that kept him out all night. But when he came home he would immediately pick a fight about alleged rumors he heard about ME!

I worked at the military PX selling Bose speakers systems; often GI's would comment about how effective I was at selling them the right electronics equipment. I was good at my sales job. The more my ex-husband stayed out all night, the more he picked fights with me. Instead of being angry with him, and expressing my hurt, anger, and disappointment; I shut down emotionally, and my sales record took a nose dive.

I knew my husband's behavior made me feel horrible, but for some strange reason instead of expressing that hurt and frustration, I checked my own behavior to avoid confrontation. Maybe I did do something out of order (military term). I was so confused by his behavior and trapped in my old beliefs systems, I began to think that I did do something wrong. I was the only American woman working in the electronics store. And all of my customers were men.

Did I do something that was inappropriate that made him angry? I second guessed every action, every move, and every conversation. I had to make sure that I was not causing the drama at home.

Deep down, I knew I had done nothing wrong. I had a 13-month-old son waiting for me to pick him up every day after work and I was 5 months pregnant!

How sad.

When did I learn not to trust my feelings?

I was about 8 years old.

More importantly, when did you stop trusting your feelings? When you can't trust your own feelings (spirit), you lose your ability to determine what is really good and what is truly negative in your life. You may begin to see good as bad and bad as good. Allow me to explain.

When you are ill, you want relief. You want a downright, bona fide cure. Instead of doing some research for a natural way to heal, you go to the doc to seek help. He/she proceeds to oblige your request for help and hands you a prescription. You look at the label and recognize it as the very same drug that was recalled and has lawsuits pending. Or, was that a magazine article….

Instead of trusting your gut, which screams, "No, there is a better way," you dismiss your own spiritual guidance and take the prescription. You even thank the doctor for giving it to you. But that small voice is still there giving hints not to take the drug.

But, you do it anyway!

Not only do you take the prescription; tucked neatly in your wallet for safe keeping, you go directly to the pharmacy without passing GO and collecting $200.00. (The Monopoly reference is poignant here because at this point you have just given over your real estate piece (the home of your spirit) to the devil. I call it prescription fiction.

You are lead to believe the promise of a cure, but all you will eventually get is more drugs, more disease, then death.

You give your power up so much, by negating the power of

your own spirit to lead; you can't trust your own gut telling you this will not fix your problem.

You pay for the prescription, take it as directed and wait for a magical response. Impatience can set in rather quickly. When relief does not happen fast, you get antsy.

Not only do you realize you are still feeling the same, but you also identify other strange symptoms, creating feelings of dis-ease and you start to panic.

Your next thought becomes, "Oh no, this is probably something serious, I may need surgery, CAT scan, XRAY... my neighbor got his leg amputated from this!"

You can't see the connection between the drug and your new concerns. Yet you do have a sneaky suspicion that your first thought to not take the drug may have been the best idea you had in a long time.

Suddenly, the still small voice (spirit) nudges you to read the accordion folded leaflet inside your pharmacy bag; and it reads clear as day, "This drug's intended use is for_____. Some side effects can include nausea, bleeding ulcer, temporary blindness, etc."

Instead of listening to your feelings and throwing the drug in the trash, where it belongs, you go back to your doc and demand that he gives you something else! The entire, time your spirit is screaming at you again – "NO Stop!"

But you don't heed the warning.

As soon as you get an inkling of a red flag, you ignore it. Instead of following your gut to seek another way, you followed your head; which is programmed in the wrong direction. Your head has been filled with imagery and propaganda to take the pill, take the pill... you've practiced not to trust your spirit.

Instead of listening to your (feelings, heart, spirit), you create a zillion different scenarios as to why you feel bad when the answer is glaring you in the face.

Your spirit is weak, but still trying to help you.

Maybe you are ready to listen. But to hear the whispers when they come, you must know what they are. Your spirit communicates with you all the time. I'm not going to go into scientific anecdotes and research abstracts, but I can tell you with certainty; your spirit is speaking even now.

Your spirit is the voice that whispers, "water- not soda" when you are grabbing your lower back (kidney region) in agony. Or the nagging feeling not to run the yellow light when you know it will turn red before you cross the intersection (the cop was just over the hill).

You don't hear it because you have completely given up your ability to trust yourself, and you fall deeper into the rabbit hole of hopelessness and despair.

Sound familiar?

You may refer to it as the "still small voice," your higher self, or even the Holy Spirit. However, you identify with it is perfectly fine as long as you begin to acknowledge that part of yourself.

I could give you a few more clues, but it would be more beneficial for you to be able to identify those moments for yourself.

What I will do is share my most profound experiences in hopes of helping you fish out hidden clues to journal your own.

CASE STUDY

The most recent memory that I can say my spirit was really trying to communicate with me was when I was in the hospital preparing for the birth of my daughter - summer of 2014. To make a very long story short... my water broke at 19 weeks. I held Melody in my body for another six weeks after my water broke. During my hospital stay, I was watching an episode of "19 Kids and Counting." That particular episode was emotionally charged for me because the wife was getting an ultrasound to see the sex of her baby. The happy moment quickly turned into a tear-jerker for the cast and me. There was no heartbeat!

Tears rolled down my face as they revealed the news to the other children and planned a funeral. The burial included a tiny coffin gently lowered to the ground by the parents. I was amazed that they were not screaming and crying as I imagined I would be. Instead, there was a reverence for the death of their daughter.

As I watched in horror, a sense of peace came over me. I wiped my tears and turned my focus to listening to Melody's heart rate on the monitor. The doctors came in the room about an hour later. They asked how I was doing; then proceeded to tell me that my precious Melody would have an uphill battle for survival.

The doctors left the room, and I said to Melody, "Sweetheart, I love you very much. My body is tired. I don't know how much more mommy can take."

A strange calmness came over me again, and I heard Melody respond, "its ok mommy, I'm coming soon, and everything is going to be ok."

You can read the entire journey from fertility treatments to finding creative ways to disguise my gray hair while proudly displaying my baby bump. Its all in the new book From Panic to Empowerment: How to embrace and angel when you expected a baby.

My goal was to hold my baby in my womb for at least 25 weeks. I was told that if I could keep her inside for another few days, there was a good chance that she would survive.

Later that evening I began to bleed… I was rushed to labor and delivery to anticipate the birth of my Melody. Then all of a sudden contractions, burning, and elation!

Melody came three days after the 19 Kids and Counting episode!

She gasped for air… they whisked her away. I watch them do all kinds of amazing things to secure her survival. But slowly she began to fade away. To hold her; my husband and I had to agree to release her from the breathing tubes.

I held Melody close to me. I must have kissed every part of her little frame. I held her tightly then finally rested her little 1lbe 13oz body on my shoulder. I needed to inhale her…

Some time had passed. When I lifted Melody to offer another kiss her skin was cool and gray. She was gone. I couldn't really cry then, I was in shock. But I did remember the calmness that came over me when I watched the Duggars bury their baby girl, and I remembered the scripture they quoted.

"Naked I came from my mother's womb, and naked I will depart. The Lord gave, and the Lord has taken away; may the name of the Lord be praised."
Job 1:21.

As sobering as the story I just recalled, the amazing part is, the Holy Spirit was with me the entire time. I didn't feel it, but when it mattered, I was able to tap in and feel my way to clarity. I was able to listen to be able to be guided.

Oh my goodness, absolutely…. I felt horrible. I felt so bad I had to continue this story in my second book; From Panic to Empowerment: How to embrace an angel when you expected a baby.

But the horrified feeling did not come over me until after I left the hospital. I was able to bath and dress my daughter even after she took her last breath. We took pictures with her. I even congratulated other mothers who had bouncy, fat-healthy babies. And yet, they were a reminder of everything that my Melody wasn't.

My Spirit sustained me. Because I was given a "heads up," so to speak by watching the episode of 19 Kids and Counting, I was able to cope. For that moment...Then I crashed.

Eventually, I recovered my spirit and mind so my body could heal. And because of that story, I am writing this for you to heal.

Learning the tips, tricks, and tools to be able to move from Panic to Empowerment seems easy enough. But it really depends first on you an understanding of yourself; your habits and beliefs.

Exploring that for a moment can have a profound effect on how you get the results you seek.

The expectation for this book is to transform your way of thinking about pain and disease. The main takeaway is to offer tools for dealing with them so you can make informed choices about your healthcare from a place of strength.

You are strong when you can choose from a place of clarity. Exploring your beliefs, their origin and whether they serve your new goals is important. But to do that, you must be able to tune in. Turn inward to examine - how you feel.

It's your feelings that will guide you to places of safety or danger- if you are not careful. But how do you do that if you are not used to "checking in?"

Glad you asked or at least thought it...

You practice!

The more you practice checking in, writing your thoughts and feelings, the more you can evaluate their place in your life to help you heal.

Let's explore your beliefs that may be having an impact on your ability to feel. Beliefs come from your childhood. They were either expressed directly or non-verbally communicated via behavior you observed. How you indoctrinate those beliefs into your life will determine how fulfilled you are.

Exploring those beliefs to see if they are serving you or not can shed light on why you are not living the life you desire or deserve. Let's look at why you are feeling pain or disease. (Overwhelmed, frustrated, etc.)

Did you know your belief system will affect your thoughts about how you live your life? Those thoughts will dictate your behaviors. Behavior is driven by how you feel.

If you feel good, you will most likely behave well. Holding doors for strangers, complimenting your co-worker on a job well done, or noticing the twinkle in your significant other's eye are signs of feeling good.

If you feel bad, you may make some costly mistakes. Being rude, short-tempered responses to simple inquiries and slamming the door behind you at the corner store is a sign that something is definitely off.

Journaling at this point may give insight on how your beliefs, thoughts, and actions drive your experience of panic or disease.   Use the current journal question to begin self-exploration. Remember to use your tools of engagement.

We haven't talked much about beliefs. We will go deeper on the subject in other chapters. But for now, just check in…
Ask yourself some questions about how you feel. See if you can trace the belief system that is driving the feeling.

I'll use myself as the guinea pig.

Lets' get back to the story of Melody, shall we?

After Melody had passed away, I wasn't sure how to feel. I was definitely numb. But when the feelings came to the surface, I was angry. I was angry at whom? At God!

We had waited seven years to have a baby. My feeling was… ok, God, you gave her to us, and then you snatched her back. You knew how much we wanted her. How could you be so cruel!?
Now instead of expecting to nurse and raise a baby, I had to learn to embrace an angel. That is not what I bargained for.

That is what I felt deep underneath my stuff (old beliefs), but I couldn't feel it right away. The belief system that was holding that emotion trapped - spiking my blood pressure up to stroke level was I'm a pastor's wife. I can't be mad at God. If I am, I'd better not show it.

Why that belief?

Well, growing up Catholic, God was to be feared, not questioned. The sentiment was, "you can feel or think it, but you better NOT say it!" (DO NOT express how you feel)!

That statement had been implanted so deep that any time I felt angry, hurt, sad, rejected... I swallowed it.

I was taught not to make waves about what was going on in our family. Keep things a secret, because someone is always watching. Always be on your best behavior, no matter what is going on. "Somebody is always watching!"

That *always watching part* had me paranoid for many years. Because of that belief system, I eventually lost my ability to feel anything. For many years, I could not even cry!

When I watched the episode of the Duggars losing their baby, and I cried, that was the glimpse of the release I'd need to heal. As I recall that moment, I can actually say that I felt a weird connection to that episode as if I couldn't stop watching because there was a lesson for me.

That was my spirit giving me a heads up on helping me deal with my own feelings.

Yes, when my baby died, I was so numb! When the floodgates opened, and I did cry; I cried for Melody and for the little girl trapped in me for all of the pain that I felt but was not allowed to express.

I remember the day I just allowed myself to go off the deep end for about 10 whole minutes. I was at the lake about to go for a walk. All of a sudden rain began to pour down on my windshield like someone was throwing buckets of water directly at me.

Then out of nowhere, I heard a scream! It startled me… it was my voice, I was confused.

I began banging on my steering wheel like a crazy person. The rain just made it easier to scream again. Understanding why I was acting like this is played out in From Panic to Empowerment: How to embrace an angel when you expected a baby; the second installment of the From Panic to Empowerment series.

My heart was broken. My spirit released me to emotionally explode under cover of torrential rain.

Nobody could hear me. So I went for it! I screamed as loud as I could… WHY GOD?!

Why did you take my baby? Why did you allow all of those bad things to happen to me and how will I ever recover from this tragedy?!

Yes, I went there!

I screamed at God, I told him I hated him, I said all kinds of stuff.

Then, just as the rain began, it abruptly stopped, and I no longer had the cover of the rain to hide my rants.
I quickly composed myself to resume my old behavior. Somebody was surely watching so I had to straighten up!

As I composed myself, the sun came out, and I felt better. Not 100%, but better.

What happened was, the rain cleansed my spirit, tears washed my soul. Not all of the issues, but enough to explore my newly discovered rage. Under my refined demeanor was a raging little girl who was allowed to be pissed! Yes, she was pissed… I was furious!

See the power that old beliefs have over you if you are not aware of what they are?

Let's fish those buggers out so you can heal. Be inspired so you can be empowered to be better and live pain and disease free, without panic and drama.

Oh, that sounds really good…yes?
One more thing…

Who's watching?

Darn it! Who cares! Let them watch, they may learn something.

Busy Bee… Is There Time for Me?

Are you busy being busy? Most of us are. Yet being too busy can have several effects on your spirit, mind, and body. If you are busy, and those activities come from a place of personal desire, and the result adds value to your life, then you are good.

But what if all the busy work is done to avoid dealing with something deeper? (Your Feelings) That is where you need to explore. Being busy is a classic method for ignoring your inner voice.

I do it, your friends do it, your parents did it, and everyone else still does it from time to time. Some of us realize when we are doing it. Others get so caught up, if you called them on it, they'd deny, deny, deny!

You can't hear anything if you are too busy to listen.

I have a technique that you may want to try. It will help you tune in to see where you are.

Sit quietly at the edge of your bed as soon as you awake. Do not get out of bed, just sit there.

Try to recall your dream (if you had one). See if you can make sense of it. If you remember it, you may want to Google a dream meaning for greater clarity.

See if your dream has significance with your current state of being or life's circumstance.

After you do that, see how you are feeling. Are you still tired, feel rested, or agitated?
Do you feel any pain or discomfort? Really check in.

Doing so will put you in the driver's seat of your day. Instead of allowing hidden emotions to dictate how things will go, evaluate them before your feet hit the floor. Take notice of them. Process them.

You will soon learn the tools to master them for your transformation to empowerment!

Chapter 5: Spirit Work: Acknowledging the Boss"

R#1-Reflection

Reflect: Reflection requires that one stop, sit quiet and check in. A quick evaluation of the emotions will give a bird's eye view of your emotional state. Emotions are the language of the spirit. Your pain or disease comes from the discomfort of your spirit.

Why is that?

We are a spirit housed in a body with a mind that thinks, and the outward expression of feeling and thought are felt in the body!

Just as your joy and vitality come from a "happy place" – spirit. Your discomfort comes from there too. If you are suffering from chronic pain or have been diagnosed with a disease; ask yourself, "...how does my spirit feel?"

The answer to that simple question will identify the 1st R.

Changing the perspective of how you view a situation, or symptom will dictate your perception of the experience being good or bad. Changing your perspective means making whatever spiritual or mental shift you need to make to get to a place of feeling good. In other words, every situation that feels bad can be for your good if you look at it differently-change your perspective on the experience. Keep in mind, this does not mean feeling good at the expense of someone else, but INSPITE of someone else.

This sounds familiar, doesn't it? Good!

This segment is a deliberate re-cap of Chapter #1: "It's You."

Even down to this quote:
"Your happiness is not found on the other side of any person, place or thing. Your happiness comes from within."~ Emily Fletcher-Mind Valley Academy

There are many clues that you may experience as your spirit tries to convey its dis-ease. Most of the time, you have not been made aware of those cues. So, when they surface, you don't automatically see them as being a spiritual issue.

Most people don't remember that they are a spirit, but only acknowledge the existence from the perspective of something outside of themselves.

Many don't believe in the spirit man that they are and view the concept as borderline superstition, fiction, and horror associated with ghosts. But whether you acknowledge that you have a spirit or not, you do.

Not embracing that part of you may be the very clue as to why you are not well. You are gently being made aware of problems, yet you ignore the warning. Eventually, the warnings become so loud they turn into chronic dis-ease.

That is why you have picked up this book. The warning has now altered your life in some way for the worst, and you are seeking relief. Are you taking multiple prescriptions to deal with many health concern, are you deliberating about surgery, or have you just gotten a diagnosis that will lead to your death?

These are all warning signs!

What if you ignored the warning of a train signal as you drove over train tracks? You may not survive to tell the story.

Consider what would happen if you ignored the whistle of a crossing guard and did not explain to your child what the signal meant? The consequence would be unspeakable. I don't even want to write it here.

I'm sure your healthy imagination would be able to create a scenario scary enough for you to go run and tell your child what the crossing guard whistle means and how they should react to be safe while crossing the street. This information would translate into a learned behavior that your child would use and benefit from for the rest of their lives.

In turn, they teach their children, and the benefit becomes generational.

Unfortunately, your experience with learning spiritual cues may be limited. There may not have been anything passed down for you to be equipped to deal with the spirit that you are.

That is ok.

It has to be.

You can start today to embrace the spirit that you are so you can use your new tools to help yourself to heal.

What's the first step?

Just keep reading.

Through these pages, I will introduce you to your spiritual self and help you create a relationship with that part of you.

Don't be afraid…

You will be amazed at how much lighter you will become. Not ghostlike, but emotionally lighter.
This is where the good stuff happens.

I'm feeling good.

How are you feeling? Check-in.

This is a good place to take out your fancy journal and pen to evaluate how you are feeling right at this moment. Go ahead, do it. This is your time to heal, take every opportunity in every situation to check in. Your heart will be better for it, and your gut will be happy as well. That next meal can go down easy when you can identify and release emotions that make you feel bad.

Have you ever heard the term, the eyes are the windows to

the soul???"

To bring things together, we will assume that the spirit and soul are same. Different schools of thought will break the concept into a very complex analysis that is not necessary for this to work here and now. If you find yourself interested in the concept further, I invite you to enroll in the seven (7) week online course, "From Panic to Empowerment: How to stop pain and disease from taking over your life by connecting spirit mind and body."

The course goes into depth about these complex ideas to help you really break free from the trapped emotions that are holding your spirit hostage from being able to communicate with you clearly. No spooky stuff, just practical exercises, and tools for exploration and learning.

Oh, yeah… how do you connect with your spirit? Right!

Well, it may sound kooky, but try this.

Go to the mirror that offers the best reflection quality. Don't use the kind of mirror that makes you appear strangely oblong or distorted. Use a really good quality mirror. All you need to be able to see is your face anyway. Make sure the lighting is good.

Now, look at yourself. Examine your face. Really look at your features: the shape of your chin, the fullness of your lips, distinctive jaw structure, prominent nose, and generational hairline. You see them?

Really marvel at what you see… I'll wait.

You are magnificent! Say it. "I am magnificent."

Repeat it a few more times until it feels real! Then, it will sound like music to your soul. You're not done yet. Now, look yourself directly in the eyes. At first, you will feel silly. You will wonder if it's ok to blink. Go ahead blink away! Then really start to focus. As you look more deeply into your own eyes, you may begin to feel an overwhelming sense of acknowledgment that "you are here."

Then, you may feel a rush of unconditional love. You may even begin to tear up.

That is perfectly fine. Have a good cry! Tears cleanse your spirit like a shower for your body. When you prevent yourself from crying, your spirit gets dirty, impeding your ability to feel...

While doing this exercise, when you do feel the whoosh of emotion, your spirit has just come to the surface and said hi. Say "hi" back and while you're there, say "I love you!" At this point, you may really begin to cry. The feeling is indescribable, scary and liberating.

Have you ever heard the term, finding yourself?

You just did.

Congratulations!

This is great progress. The key is to maintain and nurture the relationship. Getting to know your spirit man is as simple as now acknowledging the spiritual cues and learning to trust them.

Once you feel your spirit surface, acknowledge it by just saying something like, "I feel you." The more you practice and see your spirit as support on your life's journey, the more confident you will become in trusting your own feelings.

That is how you will begin to move From Panic to Empowerment because that is the power of mastering the first R in the 3Rs Approach to Healing.

Above, I just explained how to connect with your spirit, below is a list of symptoms that can be associated with spiritual illness. Some of these may seem familiar. Others may seem like they don't apply. Check off the symptoms that resonate with you and use them as journal entries. This is a short list. A more comprehensive exercise can be found in the companion workbook.

Symptoms of Spiritual Illness – Shortlist
- A lack of respect and self-esteem for yourself.
- High level of fear and anxiety
- Lack of integrity and honesty in many aspects of life
- Lack of honesty and integrity in behavior in the workplace
- A lack of spiritual activities, including prayer and meditation
- Lack of trust in the goodness of man
- The lack of courage and strength
- Lack of respect for the dignity of all individuals

Thoughts & Words Create Reality

We often do air quotes when we use someone else's words. But when we verbalize our own thoughts we often say "Don't quote me but..." Why is that we are so quick to embrace the thoughts of others, yet negate our own power to say something profound?

Not only do we not acknowledge our power to create "life," but we also deny that we have created our own disease or pain.

Words have power!

Your words are powerful. Since you are learning that power, use it for your good. Create words deliberately to allow healing.

Quotes are helpful tools that help us understand life and ourselves. Often times we create quotes that we may repeat. Some positive, some negative; not realizing that they have an impact on our overall expression of health.

Here are a few quotes you may say without realizing it... "That makes me sick, she gets on my nerves, I hate that color, and I would die for a vacation!"

Negative words can create anger. Anger makes us clench our fist in rebellion. That rebellion creates a constriction in the vessels. Vasoconstriction (narrowing of the arteries) can cause anything from a headache to a heart attack or stroke!

What words are you using to describe yourself, your surroundings, and your circumstance?

Have your words contributed to how you feel right now - your dis-ease or pain?

Using phrases like, "I don't want to get fat," is an example of how words create reality.

The word "get" is a command to the subconscious mind. It does not hear "don't," it just hears the command. The body then says, "So be it!"

See how powerful you are!?

Over the next few weeks, you will begin to see how using the 3Rs method can move you from Panic to Empowerment.

But, before you truly can embrace the simple 3Rs method you must understand the basic parts of your discomfort. Acknowledging the parts, then putting them together to work as one, is how you will create a transformational shift in your life.

Words *do* have power!

We often have people remind us to watch what we say. What we read and what we listen to can also have a profound effect on our spiritual, mental and physical health.
Over the next week, I'd like you to conduct an experiment.

Make a list of your favorite shows, current books you are reading and the company you keep. Observe the language you hear, the images you see and what you say. Ask yourself, are these experiences consistently filled with language and imagery that support a healthy you, or do they create dis-ease in your spirit.

Keep in mind, the company you keep also has an impact on your spiritual health as well. Note how you feel after you have created the list.

Will you continue to engage in those activities with those people? Or, will you choose to explore new ways to add light to your life?

What you experience in your everyday life can have an effect on your spirit. It makes sense to be mindful of what comes in. But, please don't feel like you have to make changes all in one day. Take your time. Simply jot down (journal) what you observe and make an effort to clear out what does not serve you and replace it with something better.

If you need a hint, start with speaking the truth about how you feel. If you feel sad, say so. Then follow it up with a positive quote or bible verse to move you to a better frame of mind.

> *"...weeping may endure for a night, but joy cometh in the morning." Psalm 30:5*

Now that you understand that it is your spirit man that leads you, you must acknowledge and get to know your spirit. This new relationship reinforces your potential for moving From Panic to Empowerment.

Once you acknowledge you have a spirit that is in the equation of your wholeness, it becomes easier to see how healing cannot take place until you connect with your spirit.

There was a lot of information in this chapter. Re-reading it would not be a bad idea, but you can move forward with a level of understanding if you journal some key points.

For further emersion into the content, you may want to pick up the companion workbook to keep everything fresh.

For now, see if you can reflect on the following concepts:

- Your spirit is the boss
- It speaks to you in subtle ways
- Old beliefs can hinder communication

Congratulations! You have completed your exploration of the "boss"- your spirit.

I have to admit, the content was pretty deep but easy to digest...yes?

If you don't agree, use your journal to uncover why. Are your old beliefs stopping you from gaining new ground?

Journal Entry:
Connecting with your spirit can feel like reconnecting with a long lost friend. You knew it was there on a deep level but access was restricted. How do you feel now that you have been re-acquainted?

Write something in your journal!

If so, which one(s)? You owe it to yourself to discover what holding you back from your best self. Doing this work can be the tipping point in you finally getting the relief you say you want from panic, pain, and disease.

Don't punk out now!

As a matter of fact, you can't turn back. You know too much to quit. So don't.
Turn the page to learn the good stuff.

Rewriting (reframing) your story is where the magic happens. Yes, there is magic in these pages that can be transferred to your life… just keep reading!

Notes:

Chapter 6: Mind: Rewrite Your Story

The second "R" in the 3 R's Approach to Healing has everything to do with what you are thinking. If you remember in the previous chapter, you discovered that your spirit is the "boss." Identifying what is in the spirit will determine how you can quickly see how your thoughts are driving your behavior, based on your spiritual cues.

If your spirit is low, most likely, your thoughts will follow pessimism, mistrust, frustration, a sense of; "it is what it is, I'll just deal with it the best I can."(The lies we tell ourselves.)

Conversely, if your spirit is light, you will see life's situations as a vehicle for self-discovery, learning and growing. You will be supported in this flow because you will find that positive experiences will come to you easily. Your positive vibes will create positive experiences.

Vibrations are what create our experiences; thought, word and deed. Your thoughts and words have creative power - vibration. Negative thoughts and words create negative energy- vibrations. The vibration you are putting out is the energy that will be the creative force of what you receive.

Let's look at vibration (vibes). This is a concept you are

intrinsically in tune with but may not realize it. Your vibe will attract what its familiar with. If you have a negative vibe, you will attract negative things and negative people into your life. That is a universal law! You are familiar with the universal law of gravity, right? If you drop something, it will fall to the ground! Universal laws cannot be changed. So take heed!

When you constantly rehearse illness and sickness and lack, you will get exactly that. If you surround yourself with people who have the same vibe or worse; it will be hard for you to rise. If you feel like everything around you is stagnant and dark, check your thoughts. What are you thinking? What you are thinking about is what you will create!

"According to what I have seen, those who plow iniquity and those who sow trouble harvest it.
Job 4:8

When you acknowledge your thoughts and keep paying attention to them; you may discover a thought theme. A thought theme is what you would call your "worldview." The color glass you look through to see the world around you – your perspective.

The idea of looking at the world through rose-colored glasses has been given a bad reputation. But what's wrong with that if you can create momentum in your thinking that creates vibrations of joy and happiness?

I'm not advocating for you to be oblivious to the world around you. It's easy to get stuck in the mud of gossip, world news, and celebrity drama. But, I am challenging you to create the life you truly desire. Create your own reality, on purpose.

The truth is, you are creating your reality with your thoughts all the time. You may as well get used to being in control of what you create.

Again, if your thoughts are negative, your world will be as well. But if you do allow yourself to see through rose colored glasses; you could create a magnificent life for yourself.

People who know you will be either happy with your transformation, or will find fault with it. People who used to feed off your negative vibe will become people of your past that have no place in your future. Blessing them as they leave your life will open doors for more positive experience and happier people to come in and bless you.

Ever come in contact with someone who has a positive outlook on everything, even when they are in a crisis?

You may have thought to yourself, "...this person is delusional."

Maybe you are delusional! But, if you find yourself drawn to such a person because of their outlook; it is because they are vibrating your language. Like vibrations attract.

That being the case, you can rest assured that if you are comfortable with that person, your spirit is too! If your spirit is comfortable, maybe the person you feel is delusional is one who has tapped into their spirit for guidance....

Hum.

Your spirit is saying, "Let's keep this party going."

If you are not comfortable following your feelings (spirit); instead of allowing the connection to get stronger, you get agitated. You may feel uncomfortable because your old belief system is strong. Unless you make a sincere effort to grow beyond your conditioning, you will easily slide back into your old way of thinking. But, you can drop kick those old beliefs for good if you simply make the commitment to transform your life.

Envision your future self- happy, healthy and whole; panic and disease free. Embrace that vision. Make it your life's goal to be the best you can be!

If you don't practice new thoughts, old thoughts and beliefs will return and dig deep for the long haul. That, my friend, will put you back at first base. Stop... Don't let that happen!

I know your old way of thinking has caused some of your heartache, disappointment, and fears. Yes, this may feel like a "yucky" place to be, but you've been here for so long you may be stuck. For now, you may be in a holding pattern.

Ah, but are you really stuck? There are at least two ways to look at this situation. First, you are only stuck if you believe you are. Second, you can embrace a new way of thinking as soon as you desire to. Having the right tools will create that opportunity for you.

The tool that will smash up old negative beliefs is the 2nd R in the 3 Rs Approach to Healing. It's called Reframe.

Say it With Me ... RE-FRAME!

When we tie in the concept of reframing it is usually in the context of us changing our perception of a negative feeling or experience based on our worldview (perspective).

Your perspective (how you see it) can be clouded by your past beliefs. If those beliefs have served to hold you down, make you feel bad or cloud your judgment- LET THEM GO!

How do you let old beliefs go?

I would say like NIKE, Just Do it! But that sounds so cliché.' You'd probably scoff at me anyway, and throw the book down in frustration.

I wouldn't dare get you to this point, (the good part), just to throw you such a nasty curveball. This book is here to help you catch the wave of enlightenment so you can be empowered. Not shoot you down like a new bird that just learned it could fly!

Yet, the fact of the matter is; simplicity wins here.

Even if you can't just do it (drop it). You can make a conscious decision to let go.

Then you can work on letting go.

Letting go of an old belief system is not the easiest thing to do, but there are direct steps you can take to get the process going. I will list them here so you can use them as points of reflection in your journal.

Reflection points to ponder:
Identify your belief system by looking at how you react in certain situations.

Ask yourself, where did that belief come from?

Did someone verbally communicate the beliefs to you, or did you establish it on your own through observations?

Does this belief system work for you as an adult, does it line up with your highest expression of yourself?

Can you let it go if it does not serve you?
If you can't drop it, are you committed enough to seek help to work through it?

We all have baggage…

To understand how belief systems create sticking points in your consciousness that pull you in directions you would benefit moving away from; let's get right into REFRAMING.

What is it? How can it move you From Panic to Empowerment?

Reframing is a concept that establishes the idea that there are many ways to interpret your experiences. It is the interpretation of your experiences that locks in your spiritual, mental and physical pattern that creates dis-ease, pain or bliss!

Ever wonder how 5 people can watch the same event and give five different explanations about what happened? Each person interprets the event based on their thought theme - their perceptions born out of their belief system. Because we all have a different perspective, it can be difficult to communicate our needs and get them met. Many states of disease and pain are born out of your inability to see things differently.

Over time, you accumulate emotional baggage. It's that baggage that really makes it hard to see anything but your own point of view. Not being able to see other possibilities can mess up your mind and your body.

According to Chinese medicine, emotions get trapped in organs. The negative energy of the emotions causes organs to dysfunction. Anxiety can cause a stomach ailment, rejection impacts the lungs and feelings of abandonment can cause the heart to get sick.

By now, you can begin to see that you create your own reality, based on your belief systems. These beliefs are usually set by the age of 7. Embracing this insight can help you make a mental shift in the direction of healing?

New Knowledge

From birth to seven you live in a world that is all about self-expression. You have no knowledge of what is happening outside of you and are completely in tune with what makes you feel good. You jump, play, dream and create fantasy friends. Your sense of who others are is completely tied to what they are doing for you to maintain the fantasy.

When an event happens, that shakes the momentum of your

bliss you feel shaken, disconnected from your childlike reality and you don't like it. You see the "intrusion" as a direct assault on your happiness. As a child, you are not yet developed enough mentally to see something outside of yourself. So when the experience happens, you see it as a direct hit! There is no consideration for the other players. Thus, you create your own story about what you feel, see or hear.

Since you have created your story, you can change it! You were powerful enough to create your circumstance you also have the power to change. Create something new!

If you created a story that has pulled you down, taken away your self-esteem or knocked your socks off, create again.

Let's look at this story... see how the story has created a disaster in this person's life. As the story unfolds, let's see how the character re-wrote the story (reframed it) for a comeback.

The Story
There once was a boy who lived on a farm with his family. The boy had a little sister who he was very close to. He and his sister were always together. The father was a man of few words, and the mother was very loving and caring. One day when the boy was about six years old, he noticed that his father went from saying only a few words to not speaking at all. His mother didn't seem to mind her husband's silence because she was consumed with the daily chores and taking care of the children. Yet, after some time, the boy began to notice that his mother spent less time with him and his sister and more time in a small room in the back of the house

sewing.

The less the father spoke, the more the mom spent sewing. The boy began to feel abandoned, rejected and disconnected from his family. He even stopped communicating and enjoying games with his sister.

Fast forward thirty years; the boy (man) is now in therapy with his wife trying to save his marriage. His wife explains to the therapist, "He does not talk to me or engage with the kids."

His response, "... my mom and dad stayed married 39 years. Mom stayed in her space, dad didn't have to talk. Mom took care of everything. Dad brought home the money for us to live comfortably. I take care of you and my family what is wrong with you?!"

A few years had gone by. The man and his wife were barely communicating, and the kids just seemed to be doing their own thing. The man went to visit his parents, and he asked his mom a question he held in his heart for 30 yrs. "Mom, why did you and dad stop loving each other and taking care of us? Why did you tolerate dad not talking to you and retreat to that damned back room to sew? Why did you accept that from him? Because of it, I have no idea how to communicate with my wife and kids. All she does is cry and complain, and you never complained about dad."

That man continued to tell his mom his problems and held back the part about his heart problem and a new diagnosis of colon cancer! In his mind, he felt there was no need to upset her by telling her that kind of news, yet he felt alone by not being able to share his truth.

The mother looks at her son wide-eyed. "Where did you get the idea that your father and I didn't love you and that I 'retreated' into a back room to hide from his behavior?"
"Well, that's what I saw," replied the son. "So I assumed that must have been what was going on."

"Son, how could you interpret what you saw at age 7 to come up with that (story)? Sit down! Let me explain something to you. First of all, your father and I love you and your sister with every fiber of our being. When I met your father, he was a man of few words.

When he was a child, he was diagnosed with a disease that would eventually deteriorate his vocal chords. He promised that if we married he would never let the possibility of him not speaking be a hindrance to our family. I agreed to marry your father because I loved him so much. In the beginning, we had no problems. We were very happy becoming parents, and we spent a lot of time sharing our love with you and your sister. We taught you the big picture of what family is and does. Remember family dinners, games, family chores that kept us laughing all day, but sore? We had fun didn't we?"

"Yes," replied the man, "we did have fun."

"Oh yeah, I remember mom. I actually forgot those times."

"Son, I'm glad I was able to create a space in your memory for you to see that and feel the joy of it."

"Yes, mom, I actually do feel joy, thank you for sharing that!"

"You're welcome son."

"Now, let me straighten this out for you so you can have your story clear. When you were just about to turn seven, your dad's vocal chords began to deteriorate, and he wanted to save his voice to be able to speak to us when it was most important for him to speak."

"That's why on your birthday or holidays he would sit you on his lap and talk to you about all kinds of stuff like how the crops grew, the magic of the moon and how to find good hiding places when you were playing hide and seek with your sister."

"Oh my God, mom, I completely forgot about that," replied he mad.

"It's ok son. By the time you were just about to turn eight, I had spent about 3 weeks sewing scarves to keep your dad's throat covered from the cold. Since dad could only work a few days a week, I started sewing scarves and selling them in the stores. My scarves became the fashion statement of the day."

"I made you one for your 8th birthday, but I found it buried in the mud by the fields. I just assumed you loved it so much you wanted to wear it, but probably didn't even realize you had lost it."

"I found the scarf and washed it for you. I still have it. I saved it to give it back to you all these years, but I keep forgetting to do so. Go upstairs to your dad's top drawer to the left under a white handkerchief and get it."

The man followed his mom's instruction to retrieve the scarf. As he entered the room, his dad gestured to him to give him a hug.

For the first time in years, the man felt like he wasn't giving his father a hug, but it was he who was receiving his father's love through the hug. The man felt a combination of relief, guilt, and shame.

He gently opened the drawer to find the scarf his mom had made for his eighth birthday. When he held it close to his chest, he cried. The man knew the truth. The scarf was thrown in the mud out of anger and resentment. His mother had so much love in her heart she assumed he lost it and didn't want to tell her he was wearing it to play when it was such a fancy scarf.

The father just looked up and smiled as if he knew his son was being transformed. The man grabbed the scarf, ran downstairs, kissed his mom goodbye and ran out of the door. He had to go home to hug his wife and kids. His story had been rewritten.

The Lesson
This is a fictitious story written to share a few concepts that have already been brought to the surface. We all have our own perspective, based on perception. We create a story about what we experience, yet the story may not be true.

Between the ages of birth and seven, you can only see your own perspective of what is happening in the world as it relates to your feelings of self-centeredness. Developmentally you are not able to see another's view.

Everyone creates their own story, based on what meaning is joined to the experience. That meaning will determine what the story will look like. The man in the story created his own meaning from the perspective of a 7-year-old's developmental stage. At age 37 that model surely does not fit based on that fact that he is now in marriage counseling.

After reading the story, see if you can remember times when you created a story about some event and how the story played out in your life causing you harm.

Now, see if you can reframe that story to see another perspective besides the one you have been rehearsing. By doing so, you may begin to feel relief, calmer and a sense of peace. You may even shed a tear. That is completely ok.

We cry a lot doing this work...

No worries, you can invest in a box of Kleenex for a buck at your local Dollar General.

Back to the point...

The point is- you have just discovered your power to reframe any situation that does not serve you.

You have unlocked the Holy Grail to your ability to move from Panic to Empowerment using the Reframing technique.

See how easy it can be once you understand how it works? The story was given as an example of how old beliefs can create a disaster in your life. Here is a nugget of wisdom. If what you believe about something makes you feel bad, stop engaging that belief system –stop the thought, and let it go.

If it hurts, let it go.

Letting it go is NOT easy, I get it. But here is a real-life example of how letting something go can really have a profound impact on you. Check this out!

I have a client named Betty. Betty has been coming to me for coaching and natural medicine recommendations for about 4 years. I had great success in helping her in all kinds of health issues; from thyroid to gastrointestinal problems, which are related.

The one area in Betty's life that remained a challenge was her menstrual cycles. They were always unpredictable and bothersome. Her apparent success in other areas was remarkable. Yet, this one area really began to bother me. My reputation was on the line, and my ego was beginning to take a beating.

I was building a reputation for helping people get well when western medicine was falling short. I don't feel like I was doing anything special, but I was tapping into places that conventional medicine does not.

I was teaching people how to take away what the body doesn't need and give it what it does so it could heal on its own. Whether what we were taking away bad food choices or destructive emotions we had success. Getting clients to see the value of taking minerals, homeopathic, and herbal

remedies were really getting results. When we incorporated the importance of making lifestyle changes and simply adding water to the diet, people were doing well.
Hold on, I didn't just offer water alternatives, but sometimes water was all that was needed to make a shift.

If you insist on an example; lack of water can create dehydration, dehydration can lead to headaches, dehydration can also cause systemic water retention increasing blood pressure!

Back to Betty…her case really got under my skin.

Then, as clear as a whistle, I heard my spirit say, "What are her beliefs about her period?"

I thought it was a silly question, but since I was using the mind, body, spirit language - asking was a wise move. So I asked, "Betty, what are your beliefs about your period?"

She replied, "I was taught that it was a curse from the Bible, punishment for Eve eating fruit from the forbidden tree."

Yes… she actually said it with a straight face. My response was, "Well that may have been a story told to you in vacation bible school as a child, but how true is that really?"

We talked about the logic of her holding on to that belief system and how that could be the reason why she was having so many problems with her period. I went on to explain to her that a period was an indication that she was fertile and able to conceive a child.

Each time she saw the blood that was her body's way of shedding its lining to prepare for another opportunity for conception. Birth and creation were God's design, and it was He that created us to be fruitful and multiply.

She looked at me sheepishly and said, "Oh... I didn't see it that way. But since you brought it to my attention; I can see how having an issue of blood every month could create a mental challenge creating a physical problem."

As long as she saw her periods as a curse, she had problems. When she saw the majesty of the process, her periods improved.

As shocked as I was to hear her candid response, I finally saw firsthand, outside of my own life, how a skewed perception could create disease and pain in the physical body. So I began to ask other clients about their belief systems. After some thought, I got it! A giant floodlight came on in my brain, and I understood what was missing. The light showed me the missing piece to why the majority of my clients got well but didn't stay well.

Many came back complaining about things we thought we had "fixed" via diet, mineral supplementation, detoxification, and lifestyle changes, i.e., removing chemicals from their home, using cleaner hygiene products, etc. I am oversimplifying the process. If you'd like a consult to discuss your plan of wellness feel free to book a free consult at drstephanieyhp.com/book-online

One challenge was because after clients started getting better, they would not return for follow-up visits. They told me that they felt so much better they thought they were out of the woods and didn't need me.

The other part of the equation is… after they stopped coming, old beliefs systems that were not concretely replaced, came with new ideas took up residence in their old space of the client's mind. They slipped back to their old way of thinking. The body followed!

There is a point of clarity needed here. All naturopathic practitioners intend to teach clients how to take care of themselves. The general premise is; the body can take care of itself if you give it what it needs and take away what causes harm.

It is not wise for any person to only seek help from a practitioner and not learn how to take care of their own body. You can only do that successfully when you understand the three parts of who you are; spirit, mind, and body.

Never, give over complete power to anyone and expect them to fix your life. Only God can do that. However; HE offers blessings, insight, and help from other people. So, even though you may think your doctor or health care provider is an angel, make sure they are GOD sent. Meaning, they will support you in your healing process, not make you dependent on them. Learn new knowledge, and depend on your Heavenly Father!

Visualization Meditation Smashing Old Beliefs
You've been given two profound examples of how perception and thoughts can create reality. I'd like for you to pick out a time your perception was off. Explore in your journal the

thoughts that came up. Now that you have them in your mind close your eyes.

Imagine a bright light like the Jedi swords in the movie Star Wars. Take the sword and destroy every perception and thought that was wrong and held you hostage from the truth. If the thoughts are resistant, hit them again until you can visualize them destroyed in its place, imagine a new happier thought. The new thought will support the alternate reality you'd like to embrace.

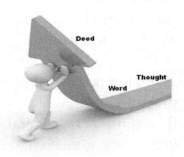

Remember you create your reality with thought, word, and deed. Thought – if it's good~ keep it, if not~ destroy it! Word- if they are empowering, repeat the create quotes and affirmations. If the words bring pain, strike them from your vocabulary and stop hanging out with people that use the language. And, stop watching shows that perpetuate the ideas associated with those words: greed, adultery, theft, abuse...

Your Magical Mind

> *"What's going on in people's lives is what's going on in people's lives because of what is going on in people minds' What is happening is what we think is happening and what is going to happen is what we think is going to happen."*
> *~Neale Donald Walsh*

It doesn't take much effort to realize that what you focus on creates momentum; that momentum produces great results. Regarding disease and pain those results are not what you are aiming for, yet, that is what you get.

The mind is a wonderful, magical organ that is very complicated. But if you were to break down the mind into its 3 parts you'd see that you have a conscious mind a subconscious mind and a super-conscious mind.

The conscious mind embodies the thoughts we know we have, based on active thinking or thoughts we notice creating mental traffic jams, making it impossible to focus. Consciously you are reading these words but are also aware of the other sounds around you. As you read, you are also conscious of your thoughts that come up as you are asked to reflect, journal or complete an exercise.

3 Levels of Experience

Super Conscious

Sub Conscious

Conscious

The subconscious thoughts are those that have a loud voice in the background of our consciousness. Just under the surface. It is comprised of those hidden thoughts that govern our automatic behavior. For instance, if you were ever bitten by a dog; subconsciously the incident created a story. Based on that story; every time you see a dog your heart may race, or you may flat out run in the opposite direction. Even though you know that the dog is not a huge Mastiff but a cute puppy fear wins.

The Superconscious mind is concerned with thoughts that you are not aware of.

They originate from the spirit itself!

Now that you have a basic understanding of the power of the mind, it's time to become more acquainted with your mind so that you can take advantage of that power.

Basic Understanding of the 3Rs Approach to Healing
The 3Rs Approach to Healing works because it weaves together the power of 3. The three tools of creation; thought, word, and deed. This concept was introduced earlier in the chapter, but further explanation can't hurt. Seeing how something works will reinforce the original introduction into the subconscious.

Clarity about how the 3 tools of creation work in your life are the strongest tool you have to turn your life around. You have to see it as a big deal and harness your power to create the health that you deserve. Your healing is as close as your own thoughts, the words you speak out of your mouth and the actions you take to move From Panic to Empowerment, using the 3Rs Approach to healing!

Connecting the Pieces
Reflect: (Spirit) Feelings are your first thought, pure thought. Feelings are the language of the soul.

Reframe: (Mind) Words are a second thought, its attempts to conceptualize feelings.
Words are the language of the mind.

Renew: (Body) Actions are third thought, an afterthought. Make Physical what we conceptualize. Actions are the language of the body.

Mental health is equally as important as physical health. You can't have one without the other. One cannot hope to be truly well without addressing spirit, mind and body issues.

Check-in.

As a naturopath, I have to interject here that mental health also has everything to do with diet, mineral consumption, and lifestyle.

These concepts will be explored more thoroughly in subsequent chapters. But, I thought to put the idea here was a good place to plant the seed for thought.

Journal Time...

Do you feel mentally well? Are you mentally well? Check off anything that resonates with you. Investigate mental health resources if you need them!
Use this brief list to check in. For a more extensive look at mental symptoms, please refer to the companion workbook.

Mental Symptoms
- Difficulty concentrating
- Poor memory
- A short attention span
- Poor listening ability
- Poor concentration

- Difficulty in learning
- Changes in an individual's analytical or processing capacity
- Dullness of the mind
- Lack of creativity
- Difficulty in sitting quietly
- Inability to confront difficult situations
- Sexual dysfunction
- Hyperactivity

Much attention has been given to the lessons relating to the mind. That is the part of us that creates the most challenges for finding peace, experiencing love, sharing the joy and giving compassion.

Your mind is what talks you out of your grand ideas of happiness when your heart is crying to be heard. I challenge you to GOOGLE a few quotes that will help you see that making the shift to deliberately putting your thoughts in their place can be the "mountaintop" experience by the end of this book. Here is one of mine.

"My mind is the breeding ground for my success"~ Dr. Stephanie Reid

It takes a lot of energy to reframe our experiences to be able to move away from the Panic Zone into the Empowerment Zone. Yet look, you made it! You are here! At this point in time, I know you are feeling free and open and alive... Right!

If you have not progressed, go back and make sure you have done the journaling exercises. The transformation lies in your willingness to do the work.

It's now time to renew...

Chapter 7: Body Talk: Renewal

One tiny five letter word can have so many meanings. We've seen in earlier chapters how perspective dictates perception and in this case even meaning. To reinforce the concept of the 3Rs Approach to Healing to move you From Panic to Empowerment, let's agree that the term "Renew" in the context of this book means "A": to make (something) new, fresh, or strong again.

[Renew *verb*
re·new \ri-ˈnü, -ˈnyü\

A: to make (something) new, fresh, or strong again
B: to make (a promise, vow, etc.) again
C: to begin (something) again

So what are you renewing? You are renewing your spirit, mind, and body - ultimately. But, the 3rd R refers to your body and its ability to heal.

Often times we take medications, undergo surgery, or try other methods to relieve our pain and disease. For a time, we may get some relief. If we continue taking prescription or recreational drugs, we become dependent on covering up symptoms, yet still, long for healing.

Healing brings peace.

What actually happens is, we find ourselves even more disillusioned as we sink deeper into a pit of uncertainty and disappointment. The only lasting way out is to find the root cause of what ails us.

What is eating at you, making you sick, and robbing you or your energy and joy? The past few chapters we explored the spirit and the mental contributors.

How much have you learned, explored, or wrote in your journal to dig deep to find your answer to the question – What is eating at you?

Getting to the root cause of those problems is what natural and alternative medicine protocols thrive on. Yet, your deliverance will require some additional work.

You will need to find the courage to look at your life in a totally different way.

That means take off the mask; look at the lies and the stories to create something... fresh!

No worries, some work is being done now.

While you were doing the activities, reading stories and reflecting in your journal, you were creating new neural pathways to healing. (Videos and fellow learner experiences are components found in the online course From Panic to Empowerment)

You see, to create a paradigm shift you have to shake things up, stop old thought patterns in their tracks and make yourself aware of things you were "blind" to.

You did that in the first half of the book when you explored the lessons: Self Exploration ~ How Do You Feel? Spirit Work- Acknowledging the Boss and Mind: Rewrite Your Story.

Now that the groundwork has been set, you will really get the Empowerment part!

In a nutshell, the "Renew" of the 3R's Approach to Healing is a passive side effect of learning how to connect the spirit and mind. The body can relax, quickly establishing a balance that creates peace and calm.

Just by allowing that to happen your heart gets a break, your adrenal gland takes a mini vacation, your bowels open... all kinds of wonderful biological functions work more efficiently.

It's a wonderful thing, really!

To be pain and disease free is a gift you can give to YOURSELF.

Anytime you need to.

Now you can truly move From Panic to Empowerment with confidence.

The key to renewal is to practice new knowledge and don't let the mind regain control.

Your Spirit is the Boss… remember?!

The Four Key Markers of Physical Health:

Sleep, Mood, Energy, Bowel function: these are the four keys to optimal health. Observing these functions of your body will put you on notice of how you are doing.

These markers are easy to identify and can be used as a personal tool for checking in. Here's the cool part; when any of the four are off, they create a chain reaction for the other three.

Look at it as if your body has parties. When all are invited- all is well. When one part lags behind, that party can't continue. To put it another way; your body works as a system of interconnecting parts and functions. When one part or system is compromised, the entire system will begin to decline.

This is a very effective system to monitor for health awareness. But, it has its flaws. The body is so efficient at working with less, you may not quickly be able to identify that there is a problem until the problem is really noticeable.

A heart attack comes to mind - cancer, diabetes or maybe arthritis. These are all of the slow burn disease states. Meaning you have to be depleted for a long time for these guys to appear. When they do arrive on the scene, you can be assured that it took a long time to manifest. Years of sleep deprivation, abnormal bowel function, low energy and funky moods can create a horrible sense of dis-ease.

But, since you have been telling a story, lying to yourself and not allowing your feelings to come to the surface; you did not hear, see or maybe not even felt the warning. And, if you had no knowledge of the four markers, then essentially you were blindsided.

To say you are healthy but have poor bowel function is like saying your car runs in tip-top shape, but the alignment is off. If the alignment stays off, you will have axle problems, brake problems, and suspension issues. Essentially your car would turn into a death trap if you did not get the original wheel alignment fixed.

It's no secret that the average person takes better care of their car than they do their own bodies. Even if you knew absolutely nothing about the mechanics of a car, you do know that every 3-5 thousand miles you take your car in for a checkup. One item that is always on the list is wheel alignment. The others include brakes, oil change, and air filter.

We already explained what happens if you let an alignment problem last too long. But if you don't get an oil change the existing oil turns clumpy and sticky and can clog up your engine. If that happens... you need a new engine. (Buy a new car)

Enough about cars, we tend to them more than we take care of our own bodies. That is the point I am making.

The standard requirement for going to the doctors for a checkup is once per year. You get a car check up on an average, once per season. If we do the math that is approximately four (4) times per year!

Now that this has been brought to your attention, it's easy to see how you may be experiencing pain and disease in your life. You have been taught to wait an entire year for intervention!

If you did feel anything, you dismissed it. Why? You learned in Chapter 4 that you are not aware of the spiritual cues that give you hints about your health. You never learned how to identify them. When they surfaced, you ignored them.

No more hiding in the darkness of the unknown. The more you know, the easier it is to make informed decisions about your health. Moving you From Panic to Empowerment is about uncovering hidden truths that can make the difference between your transformation and your demise!

Without turning this into a medical textbook, let's briefly explore what happens with your sleep, bowels, energy, and mood as it relates to health. All four components need to be working optimally for your body to function properly. Taking any of them for granted is a recipe for dis-ease and pain.

Sleep
When you fall asleep, magic happens. You repair, burn the most fat and heal! Yes, this is all possible because when you are asleep, your body does not have to be concerned with pumping extra blood. You are not running, thinking, walking or chewing. Your muscles are relaxed unless you have restless leg syndrome which would indicate a mineral deficiency.
Also, the need for calories burned for energy expenditure is

greatly reduced. That is the perfect environment for your health to be restored. But, if you deprive yourself of meaningful rest by going to sleep at 4 am when you have to get up at 7am, you can create a problem. Inconsistent sleep habits can have an effect on the kind of sleep you have which include REM and Non –REM sleep as well as your circadian rhythm. REM sleep refers to the time when you are dreaming, and you experience rapid eye movement.

Non-REM sleep is referred to as deep sleep or slow wave sleep. The quality of your sleep depends on your ability to get 3-5 cycles of both types of sleep. The quality of sleep is also concerned with whether you are following your body's internal clock or circadian rhythm.

This aspect of sleep is critical because it tells your body when it should be sleep and when it should be awake. To override these aspects of sleep can cause serious health problems. Not getting enough quality sleep is reason enough to be moody to everyone you come in contact with.

Health problems, what kinds of problems? I'm glad you asked!

Sleep deprivation over time can cause many health problems including reduced cognitive function (mental processing). According to the National Heart, Blood and Lung Institute, sleep deficiency is linked to many chronic health problems, including heart disease, kidney disease, high blood pressure, diabetes, stroke, obesity, and depression.

When I was in college, I used to pull the all-nighter study session to prepare for finals. That actually never worked for me- NEVER. I do remember the time I took No-Doze pills and drank a Mountain Dew! The point was to keep me awake so I could study. Not only could I not focus because I was literally hopping from bed to bed, but I also could not fall asleep for 48 straight hours!

By the time I could fall asleep, I missed my final because I couldn't hear the alarm. The exercise in futile studying was a waste of time and money. If my mom is reading this, she'll probably gasp!

"You did that?"

"Yes, mom I did that."

What causes poor sleep quality in your everyday life? Here are some clues.

If you tend to worry about everything, thinking about the detriment of your circumstances without thinking about solutions, you will not get any sleep.

If you eat carbohydrates before bed, you will be awake for a while. No amount of counting sheep will help. You might as well get back out of bed and do some jumping jacks to burn off the sugar (fuel) you gave yourself. Carbohydrates should only be used as a source of fuel; not a bedtime snack.

Do you want to get a good night's rest? Snack on some spirulina, it has the highest content of tryptophan- an amino acid that makes you sleep and good for building proteins. Proteins are the building blocks of every cell in the form of amino acids.

Tryptophan is needed to make serotonin, a neurotransmitter that plays a vital role in protecting you from experiencing depression and anxiety. The body also uses tryptophan to make niacin, which is a vitamin needed for cholesterol maintenance and melatonin (a hormone), responsible for good sleep.

There are so many theories about sleep, I'll keep it simple and just reiterate that lack of sleep can be costly. Don't take it for granted. One trick to see if you are getting enough sleep is to check in. If you feel like you can just get out of bed without the need for an alarm clock, your sleep was restorative.

On the flip side; if you woke up groping for the alarm clock to smack it into orbit, you have a sleep problem. If the problem is chronic, disease will make a home in your life

Bowels
Your bowels handle waste management and nutrient absorption. But let's backtrack. Digestion begins in the mouth, engages the stomach, and needs the input from the liver and kidneys before any nutrients ever get to the small intestines where they are absorbed. The large intestine is where waste is eliminated. The bowels are so critical that they are considered the most critical organ for human survival. Life and death begin in the colon!

Although we casually mentioned other organs like the liver and kidneys, I also mentioned that I was not going to make this a medical textbook. However, for the sake of common knowledge let's briefly explore the bowels.

Essentially when you chew food, saliva is the first digestive enzyme to aid in the digestive process. You must chew your food thoroughly for this to happen. I heard you must chew each bite at least 30 times. If you are not inclined to count, I'd recommend chewing until you've created a liquid paste in your mouth. At the very least, make sure you are not swallowing quarter sized bites!

After you chew for a while…

Food then goes into the stomach, necessary metabolic functions happen in the liver, kidneys, and blood. Then that "digestive soup" is passed to the small intestines for nutrients to be absorbed. If there is no obstruction from damaged villi (small projectiles that absorb nutrients), your bowels would have done their job.

But, there is a lot that can go wrong along the way. Before I go any further, I must inform you that your gut is your second brain!

What?! Yes… your second brain!

Let me explain. You need to be able to grasp this so you can effectively deal with your next health crisis. Not to be a 'Debbie downer", but the next crisis is coming.

The key is, to be able to get through the experience more quickly and not have it add to your existing blocks that grip you in panic and despair.

You should be able to do a bowel observation from the point of common knowledge and common sense.

Similar to the brain, your gut has its own separate nervous system! In fact, your gut is called your second brain. That second brain has 500 million neurons, is nine meters long and starts at the esophagus and ends at the anus. It's this brain that is responsible for mood changes, chocolate cravings and can work independently or co-dependently with the brain in your skull.

It is also this brain that can give you signals of pending doom and pleasure. Did you know your gut-brain can produce its own dopamine- the feel-good hormone?

Knowing that your gut (bowels) can do all this, it makes sense to be nice to it so it can be nice to you.

Word to the wise; be very careful what you put in your mouth!

The result can mean bliss or a battle. Personally, I'd choose to feel blissfully happy. Consider this, foods can support healing and good health or contribute to the most debilitating diseases. For instance, if you eat wheat, rye, barley or oats, which are your classic gluten foods- the entire bowel function, can be compromised. These foods create inflammation that not only hinders absorption of nutrients, but also creates a breeding ground for parasites, fungus, and bacteria.

If you are experiencing constipation, these foods are to blame. They cause inflammation, not only in the gut but throughout the entire system. Inflammation and damage to the gut mixed with microbial infection definitely equal constipation. Impacted waste is a buffet for microbes which means gastroenteritis, crone's disease, colitis and diverticulitis for you!

I warned you to be nice to your gut...

Additional waste in the body creates a toxic mess that can zap your energy, affect your mental health due to mal-absorption of nutrients and create other health problems from asthma to cancer. Think bowel irregularity is not a big deal?

Think again!

Just a side note... If you find yourself with locked bowels, using the 3 Rs Approach to Healing can help. This technique works with all kinds of stuff.

If we stick to the idea that the spirit is the boss, we loop a story, and our body follows; then it makes sense to investigate the cause of locked bowels from a spiritual angle. You have already come to know that your spirit is your emotional center. Stuffed emotions would translate into stuffed bowels. I'd surely call that constipation.

Constipation usually accompanies a stomach ache. The stomach is where your food is broken down and turned into an acid soup. If your stomach gives you a fit, ask yourself (spirit); what can't you digest or, understand?

Here is a moment to get practice. Take out your journal and write down your bowel history for the last six months. Observe if you have had problems. If so, see if you can trace them to food choices or emotions. If you can't think of anything, start today. Create a bowel log. Doing so can help you be more aware of your body functions and the changes that take place due to emotional and mental challenges. Continuing this habit of thinking will definitely ensure that you experience the shift seek.

Mood & Energy

Your mood and energy are both directly impacted by sleep and bowel function for obvious reasons. If you are not getting proper nutrients, mineral imbalances will affect your moods and your sleep.

To add additional clarity, remember that nutrients are absorbed into the small intestines. If absorption is hindered, energy gets depleted creating those funky moods I mentioned earlier. You can forget about sleep. The more toxic and less nourished you are the more likely you will suffer from some form of insomnia.

Are you beginning to see the big picture?

Think about it. If you have been depressed for some time; have you considered your second brain? What are you feeding it: sugar, cookies, soda, candy, crackers, and pasta?

I see…

If that is the case, you are also feeding your depression, low moods, and low energy.

Reviewing hundreds of hair tissue analysis over the years, I have become quite familiar with mood and energy depletion scenarios. Sodium/potassium ratios can create depression accompanied by low thyroid function brought on by eating too many carbohydrates and not enough protein.

I have seen that if inflammation exists, the body may not be able to break down protein to an amino acid form if there is inflammation caused by gluten intolerance.

The tricky part is, just because you eat a piece of chicken or steak doesn't mean you are able to absorb it. If you can't absorb it for use, it turns to an additional ingredient in your toxic soup.

I hope by now you are beginning to see a really nice web being weaved of information that can give you clues to how you can gain control over your health. Have you considered that it may be your diet that is creating your disease?

Diet is the key component to optimal health. Optimal health can be measured by your quality of life that is determined by your moods and energy. Nutrition is essential for every metabolic function. Without proper nutrition: cells can't regenerate properly, tissues become weak, organ function slows down, and you get tired. At this critical mass, pain and disease take over your life.

Your only road to gaining your health back is to get to the root cause of your pain and disease by understanding the intricate connection between your spirit, mind, and body. Once you see the connection clearly you can use the 3Rs Approach to Healing to turn your own life around; one circumstance at a time.

Do you know anything about minerals? Calcium and magnesium play a big role in your sleep. If you have a calcium imbalance, you may experience, not only dry skin, brittle nails and hair, but you will have an awful time getting to sleep. If you have a magnesium imbalance, you may experience waking up in the middle of the night and not being able to go back to sleep. This type of deficiency would also make you crave salt, which is needed to produce chloride in hydrochloric acid which is needed to digest protein.

As you can see, there are a lot of connecting pieces to your health that you may not have known about. Just knowing this small amount of information can move you From Panic to Empowerment! Knowledge is not power, the application of knowledge is power. Using this new information can be the catalyst for your transformation in 30 days or less just like this little book promises.

> **Diet is the key component to optimal health. Nutrition is essential for every metabolic function. Without proper nutrition cells can't regenerate, tissues become weak, organs don't work, you get tired.**

You can do this! You can!

Since I have so much confidence in your ability to master these concepts, let's use this section for some serious self-discovery. Get out your journal and jot down what's going on with your mood, energy, bowels, and sleep.

Review the list given and check off any health concern that you may have had over the past 3 months. See if you can connect the dots from your spirit, mind and body chapters. Identify what you can do now to stop your pain and disease from taking over your life.

Physical Checklist
- Fatigue or lethargy
- Fatigue after eating
- Fatigue at specific times of the day
- Tiredness after a normal night of sleep
- Difficulty sleeping or a restless or interrupted sleep pattern
- Grinding of teeth at night
- Drowsiness after receiving eight hours sleep on average
- Loss of sexual desire
- Impotence
- Numbness in body or limbs
- Chills and feeling cold
- Feeling hot
- Intestinal gas

Some symptoms you may be able to admit to right away. The conscious mind signals the body when something is out of balance. Some symptoms may not be realized until you read the list. You may have a remembrance of feeling "something" and all at once you may actually feel it again a day or so after doing this exercise.

When we ignore symptoms and push the reality of them out of our conscious awareness the "trigger," (word, picture, sound) activates the body to signal again.

Speak life to your body

Words have power, remember. Speak life to your body. Instead of saying, "I hate my legs, or my arms get on my nerves," say something nice about your body- something positive. Words have vibration and create life. Be mindful of the words that come from your lips. Your words do impact your health. Write something nice about your body in your journal. Say it over and over and over- until you see change. Then repeat it forever to remind your subconscious which is the boss. I'll share mine for inspiration.

> *"My body is a magnificent creation of God. He has given me everything I need to be healed. I can learn what they are to be whole."* ~Dr. Stephanie Reid

It's nice to read other people's quotes, but this is about your transformation, not mine. Create your own quote. Write in your journal. Stick it on your dashboard. Write yourself a love letter. After all, you did get acquainted with the most beautiful part of you. It's time to grow that relationship to maximize every effort to get well. Your spirit has been awakened to your consciousness giving you a new found power to ensure your transformation.

All you have to do is listen. Listen with your heart (feelings). Watch your thoughts and reinvent a new belief system. These will create a new opportunity for you to relax to rebuild and restore. You can heal and recover. You now have given yourself permission to throw out the old garment of panic that was weighing you down to re-dress yourself in a new garment of confidence stitched together by empowerment brought about by connecting your spirit, mind, and body.

Chapter 8: Spirit, Mind, Body Connected

The 3Rs Dream Team

Give yourself a round of applause. You have made it to the point where you can see that getting deep was necessary to get to this point. Have you ever heard the term "the devil is in the details?" Well getting through some of those exercises may have kicked up some stuff, but you made it here!

Congratulations!!!!

Let's recap what you have learned thus far. Your pain or disease comes from the discomfort of your spirit - Reflect. Just as your joy and vitality come from a "happy place" – spirit. Changing the perspective of how you view a situation, or symptom will dictate your perception. Changing your perspective means making whatever spiritual or mental shift you need to make to get to a place of feeling good.

Keep in mind, this does not mean feeling good at the expense of someone else, but INSPITE of someone else.

"Your happiness is not found on the other side of any person, place or thing.

Your happiness comes from within." - Unknown

Wait...

Is this a déjà Vu'? You've read this before, right?

Yes, you have. Learning new concepts is all about repetition. The more you see it, read it, experience something the more it becomes a part of you. This information can create a shift for you, but you need to internalize it. To help you do that, I stick it in various places to wake you up.

Reframing the meaning of a circumstance gives power! It creates an opportunity to re-write the old script, throw out old beliefs that no longer serve your idea of who you would like to become; if you could drop kick some old baggage. Your way of doing things that makes you happy is perfectly fine.

Do you make the rules? You should, at least for yourself.

Discomfort comes in when you neglect your spiritual health in the name of going with the status quo. God made you one-of-a-kind and unique. You know when something does not feel right. So don't go along for THAT RIDE. Choose your own route.

Renewal is the icing on this magnificent cake you are creating- a life that no longer is designed by lemons, but of colorful (healthy) cake. I used cake as a metaphor because it symbolizes celebration. Celebrate your breakthrough!

Renewal is so good because it is a passive by-product of Reflection and Reframing.

When you have successfully gotten through the first 2 Rs, you'll know it.

How?

You will feel relaxed, calm and at peace... and in Luv with everything around you. (Smile)

It's at that place that the body STOPS using its resources to deal with metabolic and biochemical issues relating to stress and shifts into healing and repair. That... is the real transformation From Panic to Empowerment. You will be able to feel it AND feel it!

With all of this new stuff going on, keep in mind that you must be vigilant that old habits don't creep in to steal your joy, burst your bubble or rain on your feeling good parade. So the biggest advice I can offer is for you to practice the 3Rs with every single opportunity you can. Heck, practice on your family members or friends; after you have exhausted your own stuff.

No, please don't go out to be a sidewalk psychotherapist. But, yes... practice your understanding of how powerful you are by employing the 3Rs Approach to Healing. By doing so, you will continue the transformational work of moving From Panic to Empowerment in not only Your life but the lives of those around you.

So now it's time... Go forth and help someone else see the light, break free.

Whose team are you on today? Team Panic or team Empowerment Choosing a side every morning is necessary because there is always a choice to make. Chose this day on what side you will give your precious spiritual, mental and physical energy to. Taking a stance can save you the stress of panic and despair.

"...choose you this day whom ye will serve..." Joshua 24:15

Putting all of the individual pieces together now offers a bigger picture of how to recover from disease and pain. After completing various activities and journal entries, you may have come to realize that integration of spirit, mind, and body is truly the key to wellness, happiness, vitality, and joy.

Get familiar with the information provided.

At the end of the book you will find a list taken from an internet source: "Analyzing the Metaphysical Causes of Disease." Use this information to identify your current symptoms and or diagnosis. Practice using the 3 Rs Approach to Healing to be able to make changes in the intensity and severity of your experience of pain and disease. Keep in mind many other variables may be in the mix. Some to consider are drug side effects, poor diet, lack of sleep, lack of emotional support, etc.

This tool is actually a cheat sheet that sheds light on the spiritual and mental cause of the challenges your experience in your body. As you become familiar with these explanations, use them to help you evaluate the 3Rs when you are not feeling your best.

From Panic To EMPOWERMENT

Journal Opportunity...

After checking physical symptoms, do some journaling. Reviewing the definitions of the symptoms, journal your revelations. Can you identify the connection between your emotions and thoughts and see how they correlate with your physical dis-ease?

Hint: Using the 2nd R (Reframe) reminds us that the way we perceive a situation is based on our perspective of it. Reframing helps you see the glass (life's challenge) as half full leading to empowerment. Panic and disease show you a perspective of being half empty. Aren't you glad your perspective has shifted!

You may be thinking at this point. "Man, I did it. I got through this little book, time for a break". Deep breath, inhale... exhale... break over! Yeah, that is all you get. You have gotten this far; you have to keep the momentum going for two very critical reasons. Let's check them out.

Reason #1: "The well of complacency."
When you learn something new, you are so excited! You feel good, and then something happens that you don't realize until you are knee deep in it. When you really want to etch something in your spirit or mind, you must practice for at least 21 days to make it a habit. Do you realize that you complain at an alarming rate? To fit in, you complain because you feel most can relate to pain and dis-ease. Can you believe we even use complaints as an icebreaker? "...that weather sure is a mess."

I challenge you to continue to write in your journal and

127

practice the 3Rs, so you won't slide back down into the darkness of despair that you worked so hard to pull yourself away from. You will know when you have slid back when you start feeling heavy, sad or disconnected from your happy spirit…uh oh. "Run Forest, Run back to the light."

I just smashed together fragmented lines from two different movies- "Forrest Gump" and "Poltergeist!"

Whatever works to drive a point home I always say…!

Please refer to the Complaint Cheat Sheet so you'll have a reference on how to get back on track. Use the cheat sheet when helping others see the value in using the 3Rs Approach to Healing. I actually prefer you just buckle down and get a companion workbook. You can download it by going to drstephanieyhp.com/shop

Reason #2: "The Midas touch."
Each time you share the information about the 3Rs Approach to Healing disease and pain you spread light and healing to the world. The healthier and well-adjusted your immediate circle of reference (people around you) the more likely your work will not have been in vain.

You see change requires a global buy-in; a collective effort. If someone you love has announced they will quit smoking, the universe is put on notice that energy is being shifted for the purpose of healing. Most likely, that person will have well-meaning friends and family to support them by removing the ashtrays, writing no smoking signs all over the house or another creative way to help the person reach the goal.

In the same way, you need support. You can gain support from others by being honest with where you are. If you feel crappy, don't say you feel fine. Speak your peace then process the emotion and work through the 3Rs Approach to Healing.

At the end of the book, I have left you a long list of physical symptoms with their corresponding mental and spiritual meaning. Use it as a blueprint for your investigation. Share the information with someone else so they can begin to see how easily a shift can make the difference between rushing to the ER or unnecessary surgery.

The sun seems to shine brighter when everyone around you is happy, even when it's raining. We call that liquid sunshine.

Thus, the Midas touch!

Stop for a journal break...

Panic & Poor Decision
There are a few more thoughts to consider before we move on. It may seem like we should have discussed this earlier, but keep in mind we were setting the foundation then. We needed to get rid of some old clothes before we tried on new ones. So, here we have some accessories for those new clothes:
- When you are in a state of panic, you WILL make poor decisions.
- When you make poor decisions, you drag innocent people into your mess.
- When you create a mess, few have the strength to save you.
- Since you created your mess, you must find the root cause on a deeper level.

- Once you identify that deeper level, you must use proper tools to clear a path for healing.
- The clear path allows others on the journey to help you.
- Sharing the transformation creates solid relationships.
- Solid relationships create happiness and joy.
- Happiness is found inactivity.
- Joy comes from God no matter the circumstance or activity.
- Spiritual, mental and physical activity keeps us alive.

"Moving from Panic to Empowerment makes every breath sweeter."
~ Dr. Stephanie

Chapter 9: Alternative Methods for a Disease and Pain-Free Life

Many alternative healing practices can be done to help you move From Panic to Empowerment, without having to resort to dangerous surgery and poisonous drugs. As a naturopath, I help clients investigate the options that may best work for them. The Western medical model is showing you that this is the right time to get back on the natural path to healing your life.

A few years ago, I can remember when doing things naturally was seen as just a "new age" experience. Time has shown us that as the number of lawsuits, medical recalls, and deaths increase, we need to be more proactive to find preventative methods for healing and wellness. Proper supplementation, quality drinking water, pure air and non-GMO foods are on the top of that list. Other options to consider are how we assess our health. The invasive measure can cause injury and death!

Technology is playing a big part in modern medicine applications. It is being used in the natural medicine arena as well. Getting blood work does not have to be your only method of seeing how the body is affected by stress. Whether, the stressor is a microbe or an environmental agent, viewing them from a non-invasive perspective can help the body heal and maintain health. A few resources come to mind that warrant a brief explanation.

Hair Tissue Analysis

Your hair is more than a vehicle to keep your brain warm or to make a fashion statement. Those locks contain hidden information about your health. Just like a rooted plant sucking up nutrients from the water of a porcelain bowl; hair follicles absorb nutrients and toxins from the blood and interstitial fluid in the scalp. That information is stored in the hair follicle.

A teaspoon of hair can tell your health history for almost 6 months. It can reveal mineral imbalances that affect everything from thyroid and adrenal function to the pancreas; liver and the cause of colitis, diverticulitis, joint stiffness to heart problems; hypertension, high cholesterol, and even infertility! Every mechanism of the body depends on the utilization of minerals. The body cannot manufacture minerals like it can vitamins, yet minerals are a critical component of every major health function. Minerals not only govern organ systems, but they are also associated with emotional health.

A Word about Minerals

Studying the work of Dr. Joel Wallach, I have come to know the importance of not just the necessity of minerals, but also the number of nutrients needed every day for the body to thrive and survive. We MUST have 90 essential nutrients daily for optimal health. If you are not getting 90 essential nutrients in the form of 60 Minerals, 16 Vitamins, 12 Amino Acids and 3 Essential Fatty Acids; you will experience a very definite slow decline in your health.

If you don't recognize the spiritual, mental, and physical cues, you can easily be debilitated by a chronic disease that grips your life in panic and fear.

Many doctors will tell you that you can get all of your nutrients if you eat from the four basic food groups. Unfortunately, that is not the case. But since millions believe that to be true, millions of people are dying each year from mineral deficient diseases that lead to death. I'm not talking about the Ebola virus or even HIV.

"Every disease that leads to death is caused by a nutritional deficiency. " Dr. Joel Wallach.

All of our chronic disease states are brought on by the lack of accurate nutritional information on the part of the consumer perpetuated by the lack of knowledge about clinical nutrition from the primary care doctor. This may seem like a trivial point, yet allow me a moment to explain.

When you experience the sensation of hunger, your brain is signaling that it needs nutrients. When you eat, your body attempts to extract nutrients from the food to carry out millions of metabolic reactions. It is those reactions that metabolize nutrients, detoxifies waste, strengthens muscles and manufactures blood, white and red blood cells as well as grows new tissue for repair. But, since our food is denatured and the soil the food grows in has been depleted via over planting and artificial fertilizer and pesticides; those basic reactions cannot take place.

The major components are missing.

We don't feel the effects right away. The body is resilient. It will repair and rebuild while on the injured reserve list. But only to the level that it can take from itself before you begin to see and feel the decline. By the time you actually feel and see the detriment, it could be too late.

There is hope! Instead of seeing this as the end, think of it as the beginning of a new you brought on by a fresh perspective thru new information. Look at that, I just reframed this bleak description into an opportunity for change.

Each day that you are blessed to wake up take a deep breath, walk unassisted, and feed yourself- it's a good day. When you can see that you can move From Panic to Empowerment with ease – it is a fantastic day!

Since you are getting closer to your transformation and personal breakthrough, let's push further. These last few pages will give you just a little bit more.

Food
As I have mentioned before, food is not what it used to be. Please don't be confused by the labels to the point that you buy anything and call it food. Food is what nourishes you, brings families together to the dinner table and grows a fetus inside the womb. Be informed, get inspired to know more. GMO's are genetically modified organisms. These foods are genetically modified to be resistant to microbes. Because they are genetically modified, any food processed with GMO ingredients will have a profound effect on your own genetic makeup. Read your labels. If it does not say non-GMO; PUT

IT DOWN!

Organic is always good, but be informed about what the label means. "Organic" generally means that the seed used to grow the plant was not genetically modified and the growing and processing did not involve the use of pesticides, hormones or steroids. Organic might not mean more nutritious unless a natural fertilizer was added to the soil. Many argue over whether the increase in price is worth it to buy organic. I say, you only get one body, err on the side of spending the extra few bucks. If organic turns out to be a hoax, then your intentions were in the right place, and you still win. As long as you thought you were eating better, you were, and your body would have responded favorably. Spirit, mind, body…

Water
There is a lot of chatter about the best water. Some say distilled is the best because it is empty. Distilled water can help removes toxins because it absorbs them as it passes through your system. Others praise the benefits of alkaline water, which can make the body Ph too neutral. The benefit supposed to lie in the fact that it demolishes free radicals which can cause cancer.

Then there is purified water and spring water. The problems with these two options are numerous. But, in a nutshell, since not all filters are created equal neither will all purified water be consistently clean. Spring water regulations vary from state to state. So there is little solace there either. My suggestion is to do your own research and make the best decision for you based on your understanding of what your body requires and your budgetary constraints to make it happen.

Air

Air quality control may seem like something out of your reach. For the most part- it is. But there are things you can do to make your home and office more conducive to wanting to take a deep cleansing breath. Air ionizer/purifiers are good choices. The more elaborate ones can be a bit pricey, but hey; what is your health worth to you?

Plants can serve as air purifiers, as well as salt lamps.

Now that you have some information use what you have to be able to create your own personal database. You never know when this stuff will come in handy or be just what you needed to know to survive a bad storm or disaster.

The list offered above was just a sample of alternative measures available to help you move from panic to empowerment. This concept of using the 3 R's approach to healing to facilitate that shift is the brainchild of Dr. Stephanie Reid founder of Your Healing Place. YHP is a natural healing center that offers hope for those who desire to get to the root cause of their health concerns. By learning about natural recourses and putting them into practice, clients learn how to take control over their health. It is because of my work with clients that the From Panic to Empowerment books were written.

You can learn more about Your Healing Place by visiting drstephanieyhp.com

Energy Healing

Traditionally, you have been led to believe that anything other than surgery or prescription drugs is less than ideal for modern healing. However, western medicine is not the only source of healing, nor is it as old as some of the most profound methods used by people all over the world.

Some strategies have been hidden, and some concepts are deliberately labeled quackery to discourage their use. When you get a chance, look up Dr. Royal Rife, one of the world's most famous pathologists. Now that is a hidden story that will knock your socks off. His medical breakthroughs were discovered in the 1930s. Because Rife was not the mainstream, he was shunned, locked away, and died poor. Rediscovering his accomplishments is changing the face of healing for the better.

Have you heard about healing frequencies?

Emotional Clearing
Emotional clearing is a very significant aspect of getting to the place of wellness, spirit, mind, and body. Dr. Brad Nelson is the trailblazer in that field. Basically, Dr. Nelson has created a way to remove emotions trapped in the body that may be causing disease. Going into a long explanation would ruin your new found skill of self-discovery. So, I admonish you to do research on all ideas that are new to you.

My primary intention was to teach you that you can move From Panic to Empowerment by learning the 3 Rs Approach to Healing. I believe I have delivered that to you in a way that is easily digestible and duplicatable. Meaning- please teach someone else!

Technology for the New Age of Healing
Nano SRT Bio Scan is a device that not only detects stress on

every organ, bacteria, DNA, muscles, mycotoxins, food additives, household cleaners, and environmental stress; but also your emotions. It can even reveal what colors are causing stress. This device works by getting a reading on the stress of the subject (in various categories) by using frequencies and vibrations detected through the skin. Because of this technology I fit into the STEM category of professions that helps to change the face of healing.

Everything in the environment is vibrating, even you and your organs. If the vibration is low, that will mean low energy, low vibrating energy leads to dis-ease.

High vibrations create wellness!

Everything is vibrating.

Here is a powerful thought to get about vibrations - You can feel it!

Yes, you can. When someone is in a bad mood, you can feel it. The person is vibrating low energy. The longer the person stays in a low vibrating state, the more easily they will be susceptible to the manifestation of dis-ease.

Think about it; you catch a cold, flu, STD because you are vibrating on the same low vibration of the energy of the dis-ease.

If you are already in low vibration and you connect with another person that is also in a low vibration, you will be more likely to have a pity party or gossiping session.

You two will most likely gravitate to each other creating a bond of misery.

You two will most likely gravitate to each other creating a bond of misery. You have heard misery loves company.

Those types of relationships will eventually become a burden; usually for the one who is seeking relief. Or, become a sore spot for the person making strides to a higher vibration.
If you are feeling bad, recognize that you are vibrating low energy. Notice others will either stay away from you or get into an altercation with you because the two conflicting vibrations will clash. If your relationships are suffering check your vibe!

Keep in mind that everything has vibration, even colors. Using your environment as a healing strategy can have a profound effect on your health. There is no accident that restaurants have a lot of red and hospitals have a lot of muted blues.

Being aware of colors and their meaning can have a huge effect you how you feel. Be mindful of what colors you wear, choose your vehicle, shoes, even color for your bedroom and towels carefully.

Being able to check in will make the difference between mental clarity, agitation, excitement or drain on your energy.

The Zyto Scan
The modern application old technology is what's used in the natural medicine field. Its importance for healing is becoming more and more relevant. Invasive procedures create

discomfort, increase rates of infection and can maim or kill.

It makes all the sense in the world to investigate the options available so you can make informed decisions. If you can be tested for infection without giving blood; why not?
We've already seen that everything is vibrating; now we can show that energy medicine is a viable option as well.

Oh, Sorry...

I got ahead of myself. We were talking about the Zyto scan. What that does is scan your body for biological preference. Just by reading the energy from your palm and scanning your vibration against vibrations of remedies, vitamins, herbs; it can be determined which products will be good for you.

That may sound creepy. But the way you are treated now is usually by trial and error.

You know how it goes...

Your doc asks you a few questions (relying on you to recall your symptoms) based on what you say and maybe a blood test, you are given a prescription drug. The recommendation is for you to try it for a few weeks to see how it makes you feel. Often times that feeling will be magnified and not cured and additional prescriptions will be offered. This is all based on your words, the doc's educated guess.

Using the zyto negates the need to ask you anything verbally. You are asked thru the scanning process. The device scans your palm and from your energy pattern is able to determine what services and natural remedies you would best benefit from.

Yes! That is cool!

If it sounds a little far off for you then consider the technology you take for granted that 20 years ago only appeared in sci-fi movies?!

Do you have a cell phone, face chat or listen to music through your car via your cell phone playlist?

I rest my case!

Being able to move from panic to empowerment will require you to have an open mind about what is possible. Hopefully, learning how to reframe your thoughts will help you embrace new possibilities for your own good.

If you truly want to take control of your life, you must be willing to get out of the insanity trap.

Doing the same thing over and over, expecting a different result is insanity!

Here is a list of new sources of healing. Learn more, teach you, take some classes about:

- Water
- Air
- Food
- Minerals
- Energy Healing
- Emotional Clearing

- Technology
- Colors

Chapter 10: Dr. Stephanie's Story

My story begins with confusion and ends with gratitude. I would imagine many of us begin life this way. So many twists and turns. So many personal stories intertwine with ours. Losing track is easy. Where does your reality begin and your true living begin?

By passion, I am a naturopath and an empath. I often wear my heart on my sleeve more often than I like to admit. A naturopath is one who seeks to help others heal by encouraging lifestyle changes: nutrition, breathing, emotional clearing, yoga, massage, etc. Naturopaths also have a command on the subjects of anatomy, biochemistry, biology and many other fascinating topics. That's why they can be the most helpful health practitioners you can find. They will most likely be the go-to people for real information on not just how to use herbal remedies, vitamins, minerals, herbs, and nutrition; they can help you do it right, so you don't waste valuable time and money.

An empath is one who has the gift of feeling other's emotions. Sometimes this can be a useful tool for helping clients express their feelings for spiritual and mental healing. However, with this gift comes darkness. The challenge to not allow the emotions of others to pull me down can get sketchy at best. It can be difficult to determine if the emotions coming in are mine or the clients. That can mean a double stress overload that leads to many health problems. I've had my share of heart problems, respiratory problems, lupus diagnosis and asthma.

As I embark on almost 51 years of life, I find that my beginning story is what brought me to this moment. It's why I do what I do, why I have written this book.

If you read the introduction, you learned that I am passionate about helping people see a better way. I like to think I offer hope to those who have lost themselves in the loop of panic and frustration. I don't have all of the answers. But I can say that some truths have come to me through just being alone, meditating or doing creative work. So, I've shared them here.

I spent 6 years exploring spiritual concepts and truths through study and using the modality of therapeutic massage. The body tells so many wonderful stories about a person's life. It also harbors some of the deepest hurts. As I was able to release those spiritual blockages from many bodies, I came to understand the spiritual connections and how they affect thinking, behavior and physical expression. I discovered a gift I didn't know I had. I feel people's emotions! I discovered that I could read the energy that escaped as if I saw the story as it lifted from an emotional hiding place.

Sometimes, I was mortified by what was revealed. Other times, I felt honored to be able to get a glimpse of the true nature of man. Naked massage clients said more to me asleep than they would ever verbally articulate. The more I massaged, the louder the gift became. It got so loud at times; I would tell the client what I heard. To my shock, they would jump up and ask..." how did you know that?" I would always defend myself by first stating, "I am NOT a psychic, and do not ask me anything about your future!"

They'd look at me wide-eyed as I'd sheepishly try to change the subject to something lighter.

It was those profound moments I questioned why I existed. Why was I here? Where did this strange gift come from, and how do I use it?

I have been told that I was born in an adoption agency in Philadelphia, Pa. I was bald with two tiny teeth. My mom was raised by her grandmother, a devoted Roman Catholic. (I emphasize Roman because it was emphasized to me as if it were a badge of honor.)

I could imagine that having a granddaughter, unwed and pregnant was really frowned upon back then; especially with the Roman Catholic guilt attached to it. I can see that the logical thing to do was to go away quietly and give me up.

Well, the plan took a detour! Mom gave birth to me but didn't give me up. As she recants my birth story, she tells me that I did have parents ready to adopt me.

Apparently, they had been trying to conceive for many years without success. So, adoption was their only hope. Imagine that, I was someone's only hope. Ironically, I was the only hope for three longing souls. My adopted mom and dad as well as my birth mom!

Wow, such a heavy burden on a new soul. Or is it?

Maybe not...

A soul knows its intention before conception and birth. I explain that concept using Melody's birth and death story in the new book. Melody came to me as a vision which I explain in chapter #1 of From Panic to Empowerment: How to embrace and angel when you expected a baby. She clearly spoke before conception. That is spiritual communication at its best.

If you'd like to know more about the topic, go to frompanictoempowerment.com. You can also get a copy on Amazon in paperback and in Kindle form.

Ok, let's stay focused...

After writing about Melody, I came to realize that my soul has a mission. Yours does too. Sometimes a life-changing circumstance has to shake you up before you can see it. Even then, a process of unfolding must take place.

It's a progression. When I look at how my life progressed I realize my mission is to be an intercessor; a-go-between, to help people see the possibilities of their circumstances.

Back to my story...

According to mom, she gave birth to a baby that was dead!

The nurse said, "I'm so sorry" and whisked away a lifeless form. Mom recalls a doctor saying, "Something is still attached." They pulled me out; mom just stared and cried.

The nurse asked her why she was crying. (Seriously, does one really have to question tears a time like this?) She replied, "I want to keep my baby."

Stop!

You may be thinking. What a wonderful story. Consider this. Because my mom made a decision from the perspective of a 15-year-old, she was not equipt to make such a profound lifelong decision without the benefit of sound counsel and a plan. She had neither.

However, I chose her, my spirit did; and for that, every experience up until the day I wrote this book was part of God's plan for the reason my soul incarnated into the body. I have endured a lot! Will the rest become a New York Times Best Seller? I have to write it first. But for now, I suggest you read every From Panic to Empowerment book that comes available. There will be words of wisdom and tools for transformation.

This concept can get deep, that's why I encourage you to read the second book-From Panic to Empowerment: How to embrace an angel when you expected a baby. It will answer hard questions about mortality and hopefully offer peace to your heart if you are grieving over the loss of a loved one.

The nurse (nun) asked her was she sure, and mom said, "Yes, but I'm afraid."

Of course, she was afraid.

She'd have to go home with a bundle, and now the secret

would be revealed. The plan to go away quietly was ruined, mom would become the talk of the neighborhood!

I'm sure that my mom was not the only teenage unplanned pregnancy in a community of staunch Roman Catholics.

But, she was definitely the one that would stick out.

There is so much more to share. Continue to look for new From panic to Empowerment books. For now, let's just say; my life's purpose is to give hope.

That's why I can do what I do now. I wrote these chapters so you could have a compelling story to give you hope. TPS-tell a passionate story is what they say! Hopefully, my story was passionate enough to inspire you to journal and discover your own passionate story. You may find that your life has a deeper meaning than you thought and the lessons are to be shared to help someone else move from Panic to Empowerment.

Conclusion

To recap, this little book was written actually out of frustration. You see, I wholeheartedly believe in the power of the body to heal itself. To that end, I do whatever I can (within my scope of work) to help people get well.

No, I do not claim to cure anybody. What I do is find creative ways for people to see their own participation in the disease or pain process and offer them tools to make changes so they can help the body heal on its own.

Before embarking on the concept of the 3Rs Approach to Healing, I did what any health practitioner would do. I'd ask a lot of questions about physical symptoms and tested for solutions. People got better, but relief was short-lived.

That really burned me up.

So, I started analyzing files to search for a common thread. When I found it, I felt like I had invented the light bulb. The only thing I had done was use my thinking cap to see things from a different perspective.

Once, I got the message, my mission has been to change your perspective- teach you a new way to look at disease and pain so you won't ever have to blindly go into a panic fit when life throws you a curveball. Let's look at this honestly. You have already had a few curve balls knock the wind right out of you.

We all have.

I've shared my Melody story and the story of my sister. Those two losses really took my breath away. But guess what, I used the 3Rs to bounce back, and now I am making a sincere effort to bring you with me.

I am so passionate about this movement; I created an online From Panic to Empowerment University! It's a platform that helps you do deep self-exploration and discovery to achieve your best self.

You can test the platform and take an introductory course for free at drstephanieyhp.com/fpte-univerisity.

There is already a lot of information out there on this subject. But, I believe nobody delivers it like me, and God gave it to me to share. Even if only one person is helped, the effort to make this dream of writing a book a reality was well worth it. In fact, this is the second edition of this publication in less than 18months, and there is already a new book in the series. From Panic to Empowerment: How to embrace an angel when you expected a baby. You can find it on Amazon!

I challenge you to find something that you feel is worth it. Something you always wanted to do. Then just do it.

Yeah, I hear ya...

I'm saying go do it as if this is easy.

It can be - if you believe it to be so. Even if you think just doing it may be hard, reframe your story about the hardness of things.

Explore who told you that. Shatter the thought and forge ahead toward your bliss. Reach for the thing that empowers you; then soar like a rocket into space! When people made me feel like I couldn't do something, I'd say "Watch my smoke, don't choke on my dust!"

Translation: Your negative vibe will not stop my momentum. And... if you continue to get too close, you may get hurt!

I meant it!

Do you mean it?!

If you do, your next step is to really master this new information. Enroll in the course and be a trailblazer in not just freeing yourself, but also free someone else

Doing so will prove that you are "there."

Where is there? Where ever you want it to be.

Higher than you have ever been before!

Hold on, I know you're feeling really good right now, you've connected with your spirit, mind, and body and you know how to use the 3rs.

Great!

But you must practice; or else, the good stuff you learned will go straight out the window like the information you thought you learned from your last book. If you practice, your old life will seem like your ancient past. If you don't, you will get drop kicked backed to your sad old existence, and it won't be because I didn't try to help you.

Just in case you're not sure how to move forward, I added a magnificent tool I found on the internet. In the next section, you have the opportunity to look up your ailment and see the emotional connection.

If you want to know more about your subconscious emotions and how they have a physical impact on a technological perspective schedule a zyto scan. The technology allows me to see your trapped emotions, where they are stored and what remedy to use to heal the damage caused by their existence. If you have a bladder problem, I can see the emotion that is trapped in the bladder and the appropriate remedy needed to heal the problem. The spiritual and mental root is addressed by implementing the 3 Rs Approach to Healing tool.

You have been completely bombarded with everything that pulls you away from healing and toward dependency of thins that don't work well. I am determined to give you every resource to heal.

Now that you are at the end of the book, what's next? Reread every chapter, and use the companion workbook found at drstephanieyhp.com/shop. The file is downloadable and fillable, making it the perfect tool to track progress.

If you are serious about your transformation From Panic to Empowerment, you will read this again. The next time you will be able to connect with the content to use it as a life tool as it was intended. Each time you read it, you can see how your responses change in the workbook.

Practice Makes Life Better
Analyzing the Metaphysical Causes of Disease

Directions: Use the information below as a tool to help you practice the 3Rs approach to healing.

Using the list identifies your physical disease or pain. Review the spiritual/ emotional connections.

Reflect: See if you can identify the origin of that emotion/ feeling.
Reframe: Practice reframing your old perception by changing your perspective.
Re new: Jot down physical changes just by doing the 1st 2 Rs

Acne: Outbreaks of acne denote an eruption of pent-up emotions. On a deeper level, it means that you are not accepting yourself and have low self-esteem. It is common for teenagers because they are sensitive are in the process of defining themselves. The metaphysical cause of acne can be altered by changing negative thoughts, accepting yourself as you are and admiring yourself for your inner beauty.

AIDS (Acquired Immune Deficiency Syndrome): This serious disease is prevalent in those who are unable to love themselves due to low self-worth and use sex to create an illusion of love.

This dependence on others inevitably leads to disappointment and gives rise to guilt. The self-depreciation leaves one with no inner peace. Thus, it necessitates the need to love and accept the self with an open heart.

Arthritis: Arthritis, Rheumatism, and Osteoarthritis are rooted in self-criticism, self-rejection, and buildup of resentment. These issues can also be caused by inflexible thinking, having difficulty asking others for help, deep resistance and inability to forgive someone. The spiritual meaning of this disease, particularly Juvenile Rheumatoid Arthritis is associated with lack of support by parents and a fear of being alone.

Asthma: It is indicative of fear, anxiety, unresolved grief, feeling stifled, and wanting to take on more than what you can handle.

Autoimmune diseases: Autoimmune diseases include Lupus, Meniere's disease,

Multiple Sclerosis, Scleroderma, Psoriasis, Alopecia Areata, Crohn's disease, Celiac disease, Addison's disease, Grave's disease, etc. More often than not, these issues are the result of self-bitterness, self-conflict, and self-hatred due to some guilt.

Bedwetting: the Metaphysical reason behind bedwetting is systematic suppression of a child by an over-dominant parent.
Cancer: It denotes longstanding resentment for the past and emotional wounds. When dealing with this debilitating disease, it is advised to forgive yourself as well as others for

all the sufferings that you have endured.

"A bodily disease may be but a symptom of some ailment in the
spiritual past."
– Nathaniel Hawthorne

Colic: Mental irritation and impatience are believed to be the spiritual reasons underlying this condition.

Common Cold: This common ailment is usually related to confusion and disorder.

Constipation: It is caused by the fear of future and holding on to old ideas/feelings for longer than required.

Depression: Spiritual interpretation of depression is anger, disappointment, emotional pressure, and withdrawal from life.

Diabetes: It is a metabolism disorder. The metaphysical cause of Diabetes is emotional isolation and lack of sweetness in life. There is a feeling of bitterness in the world. Type 1 Diabetes or Juvenile Diabetes denotes an inner emptiness.
Type 2 Diabetes or Adult On-Set Diabetes indicates self-rejection and guilt on account of blaming yourself for not being able to help others.

Diarrhea: Metaphysical causes of disease like diarrhea are indecision and worry. It can be the result of trying to escape from something or someone. It is also associated with a poor self-image.

Dizziness: It is caused by fear, anxiety, and scattered thinking;

especially when you do not want to face a situation.

Eye Sty: The spiritual meaning of <u>eye sty</u> is suppressed anger and anxiety.

Fever: Regarding metaphysics, <u>fever</u> denotes anger which, in turn, gives rise to heat and an increase in body temperature.

<u>Hair Loss</u>: It signifies that you are seeking too much control and not trusting the natural flow of life.

A headache: the Metaphysical cause of <u>headaches</u> is usually self-criticism and internal conflict.

<u>Heart disease</u>: It shows that you take everything to heart and have low self-worth as you tend to deny your needs and focus more on others' needs. Thus, the meaning of heart disease is emotional exhaustion and fear of being unloved.

<u>High Blood Pressure</u>: It is caused by repressed anger or grief. Simply put, it is an accumulation of the inner pressure. Individuals suffering from this condition experience difficulty in trusting others, even themselves.

"If someone wishes for good health, one must first ask oneself if he is ready to do away with the reasons for his illness. Only then is it possible to help him."
– Hippocrates

Insomnia: <u>Insomnia</u> represents negative thoughts, worry, and lack of trust, fear of death or fear of accountability.

<u>Irritable Bowel Syndrome</u>: This chronic gastrointestinal illness is related to a victim mentality, anxiety, and refusing to

take charge.

Kidney Stones: Metaphysical meaning of kidney stones is unresolved grief that you have been holding on to; solidified emotions. While analyzing the metaphysical causes of diseases, keep in mind that the right side of the body is associated with physical energies whereas the left side is associated with emotional energies.

Liver Problems: Liver problems like cirrhosis and hepatitis are caused by suppressed anger and rage. It signifies an attitude of resistance to change. Liver cancer is related to chronic fault-finding, whether to yourself or others.

Motion Sickness: It represents a lack of trust and fear of losing control.
Nausea: Metaphysical meaning of nausea is undigested ideas and negative emotions.

Obesity: It depicts that you are putting distance between yourself and the world. This disease related to the fear of feeling humiliated or ashamed.
It points towards the fact that you find it difficult to say no to others and hence, take on more burden. In an attempt to please others and make them happy, you tend to neglect your own needs.

"Happiness is a perfume you cannot pour on others without getting
a few drops on yourself."
– Ralph Waldo Emerson

Pain: Pain represents emotional guilt, tension, and fear of moving forward.

<u>PMS</u> (Premenstrual syndrome): It is a result of having conflicting emotions and resentment about being female; unwilling to flow with nature.

Psoriasis: It represents excessive fear of being hurt due to damage to self-esteem in the past. <u>Psoriasis</u> is also associated with self-hatred and the belief that you are not worthy of being loved.

<u>Skin Disease</u>: Spiritual significance of skin problems is that it indicates that you are being overly sensitive, or being out of touch with others or yourself.

Slipped Disc: Experiencing difficulty in making a decision is the most probable metaphysical cause of this ailment.

Thyroid Disorders: Frustration due to an inability in expressing yourself emotionally. Hyperthyroidism is caused by fear of responsibility and selfishness. <u>Hypothyroidism,</u> on the other hand, is the result of feeling repression or hopeless.

Tooth Decay: <u>Dental decay</u> and cavities are the results of taking life way too seriously. It depicts your inability in accepting a situation in life due to anger.

Ulcers: They are often related to inflexibility, fear, stress, and anxiety owing to unresolved issues.

Metaphysical causes of disease are rooted deep in the energetic structure of the universe. They assist you in improving your perspective through introspection.

Moreover, you must have noticed that most of the diseases

listed above are associated with anxiety, fear, and anger. No wonder, "stress" is a common cause of illness.

Practice may not always make perfect, but it will sure get you closer to the mark." Dr. Stephanie

References

Gut instincts: the secrets of your second brain. (2012 December 18) Retrieved from Neuroscience: articles and news from the latest research Reports: http://neurosciencestuff.tumblr.com/post/38271759345/gut-instincts-the-secrets-of-your-second-brain

Kurus, M. (n.d.). Check Lists for Physical, Emotional, Mental, and Spiritual Health. Retrieved from MK Projects: http://www.mkprojects.com/fa_checklists.htm

Metaphysical Causes of Disease. (2012, March 23). Retrieved from Home Remedies & Natural Causes: http://www.speedyremedies.com/metaphysical-causes-of-disease.html

Lynes, Barry. *Rife's World of Electromedicine: The Story, the Corruption, and the Promise.* South Lake Tahoe, CA: BioMed Pub. Group, 2009. Print.

Wallach, J. D., & Lan, M. (1999). Dead doctors don't lie. Franklin, TN: Legacy Communications Group.

Walker, N. W. *Water Can Undermine Your Health!* Print.

Walsch, N. D. (2007). Home with God: In a Life That Never

Ends. Atria Books.

Watts, David L. *Trace Elements, and Other Essential Nutrients: Clinical Application of Tissue Mineral Analysis.* Place of Publication Not Identified: Publisher Not Identified, 1995. Print.

Technology Resources:
Zyto Scan Info: Zyto.com
Bio-Scan SRT: http://www.ihtbio.com/ihtblog/bioscan-srt/

Made in the USA
Middletown, DE
02 February 2019